"Why Do Only White People Get Abducted by Aliens?"

"Why Do Only White People Get Abducted by Aliens?"

Teaching Lessons from the Bronx

Ilana Garon

Skyhorse Publishing

Skyhorse Publishing books may be purchased in bulk at special discounts for sales promotion, corporate gifts, fund-raising, or educational purposes. Special editions can also be created to specifications. For details, contact the Special Sales Department, Skyhorse Publishing, 307 West 36th Street, 11th Floor, New York, NY 10018 or info@skyhorsepublishing.com.

Skyhorse® and Skyhorse Publishing® are registered trademarks of Skyhorse Publishing, Inc.®, a Delaware corporation.

www.skyhorsepublishing.com

10 9 8 7 6 5 4 3 2 1

Library of Congress Cataloging-in-Publication Data is available on file.

ISBN: 978-1-62636-113-3

Printed in the United States of America

For Mom and Dad, my first teachers.

Table of Contents

Conclusion

Author's Note

The names of the people that appear in this book have been changed in an effort to protect their privacy. If any names are similar to those of actual individuals, this is purely coincidental. I also made an effort to protect the identity of the institutions featured throughout these pages. All events described are of my own memory.

Throughout this text, I have incorporated journal entries that I wrote during my first few years. In 2003, when I began teaching, blogs were not yet popular—instead, I sent these entries by email to a growing group of family, friends, and colleagues who were interested in learning more about these experiences.

Prologue

What This Book Is and Isn't

He stood in the front of the classroom, punching his fist against the palm of his hand.

Smack. Smack.

I was in the back of the room, bent over the desk of one of the students, so I didn't notice when he entered; then I stood up, and there he was. He wore a baggy hooded sweatshirt that covered his head entirely, like the cloak of some monastic order. His body was angled away from me. I couldn't see his face.

"Who are you? What are you doing here?" I asked him, startled.

No answer.

My ninth-grade students, suddenly silent and alert, were looking up at our intruder with puzzled expressions.

"Okay, give me your ID."

"F— off," he said.

"Give me your ID! *Now!*"

Apparently, he hadn't found whomever or whatever he was looking for. Without another word, he turned and moved toward the door.

I ran in front of him and blocked the entrance to our classroom with my body. He was at least a head taller than I was. I was scared—partly because he had shown me such casual disregard when I'd asked for his ID and partly because it unnerved me that I still couldn't see his face— but I was compelled to stall him anyway, because I couldn't lose face in front of the kids. I had asked him to do something, he had disobeyed me, and they had watched it happen; my already limited authority was at stake.

"*Security!*" I called into the hallway as loud as I could. I hoped that the school police stationed in our school would, for once, appear at the right time. They were constantly interrupting class to check if the students were wearing do-rags, but when you really needed help, they never seemed to be around.

"*Security!*"

The intruder body-checked me against the doorframe, shoving me aside. My arm smacked against the wall, hard; I was vaguely aware that I would have a bruise later. Instinctively, I grabbed his sweatshirt and tried to hang on, but he shook me off with little difficulty and ran out of the room and straight into the stairwell ten feet away. Before the stair-well door slammed behind him, I saw that he was heading downstairs.

Without thinking, I ran after him. As I took the steps two at a time, it occurred to me that I didn't actually know what I would do if I caught him. Above me, I heard my students screaming.

"Miss Garon! Come back! Don't do it—he's Bloods!"

Bloods. That hadn't occurred to me, though it probably should have; of the several gangs that had members in our school, the Bloods were the most prevalent. I stopped in my tracks. He was out of my sight, and I could no longer hear his footsteps—I knew I'd never catch him. And now, my students' anxious voices brought me back to reality. What the hell was I doing chasing a gang member down the stairs?

I turned and walked back upstairs, out of breath. My face burned with frustration and embarrassment. One of the boys, Carlos, met me in the middle of the stairwell.

"Miss, it's okay to cry," he said. He put his arm around me.

But when asked later to describe the intruder, the students were tight-lipped.

"How did you know he was Bloods?" a security officer asked them fifteen minutes later.

No answer. Several of the students busied themselves picking at graffiti on their desks or biting on their pencils. All they would offer was that he had a black sweatshirt, was either black or Hispanic, and was "mad gangsta."

"That describes the entire school," the officer told me.

———————

This is me: I'm a five-foot, five–and-a-half-inch Jewish girl who weighs 135 pounds on a bad day. I have a curly ponytail, freckles, and Harry Potter glasses. I like running, swimming, independent films, popular history, and reading. I wear lemon-scented body spray. I compulsively say things like "Oh, for the love!" and "No shit, Sherlock!" and "Okay . . . here we go." On my wall, I have a poster showing the genealogy of all European monarchy since 1000 AD.

My students will tell you I am the whitest person they've ever met.

I grew up in Falls Church, Virginia. My family moved to France when I was two, and my three younger brothers were born during the five years we spent in Paris while my father was working for the International Energy Agency in France. We moved back to the States when I was seven years old, at which point I was enrolled in a private Jewish parochial school.

This is the school I went to: In addition to our "secular" subjects such as math and English, students in seventh grade and above took daily courses in Bible, Rabbinic law, Hebrew, Jewish history, and theology. We attended nine periods a day, not including lunch. After school we played sports, edited literary magazines, and performed a mandatory eighty hours of community service by graduation. I went through twelfth grade there.

Our school was strict. If you were late to class three times, you had lunch detention. After two lunch detentions, you had an in-school suspension, which would take place on a Sunday. An unexcused absence to any class would result in the AWOL student's parents being phoned, a total loss of credit for any work done that day, and a 3 percent deduction from one's marking period grade.

The 3 percent deduction was the clincher—that could make the difference between an A– and a B+. For students who had been groomed since birth to follow family legacies at Ivy League schools, this was an unthinkable penalty.

Myself, I never got further than lunch detention, which I acquired several times for being tardy to various classes. The first time it happened, I sat in the detention room eating my sandwich and crying. The math teacher monitoring the detention room that day came and sat down next to me.

"Why are you here?"

"Because I was late to Bible class—my locker's on the other side of the school."

"Is this your first time in detention?"

"Yes."

She burst out laughing. "This is good for you," she told me, as I stared at her with red-rimmed eyes. "You're not a detention virgin anymore!"

———————

This is what you will learn if you watch *Dangerous Minds*, *Lean On Me*, *The Freedom Writers*, or any of Hollywood's other takes on inner-city education that have been released over the past fifteen years:

1. The problem with inner-city schools is that most of the teachers don't believe in their students' potential. A bright-eyed, newly minted teacher who "believes" is all that delinquent kids need to do a 180-degree turn around and gain admission to Harvard.

2. You will have no more than fifteen students in a given semester, and the first time you raise your voice at them, they will all suddenly realize you mean business and cooperate.

3. You will know a school is an underfunded, gang-ridden cesspool if there is graffiti on the desk, loud rap music playing in the hallways, and . . . gasp . . . crooked window shades!

———————

When I first saw *Dangerous Minds*, I was twenty-three and had already been teaching in the Bronx public schools for a couple of years. My friends back home in Virginia had rented the film, figuring I'd appreciate it.

"So is that just like your life, Ilana?" they asked, when the lights came back on.

"Well, kind of," I said. "Except for the fact that I teach 150 students a term, not 15; that I compete for attention in the classroom with mice and cockroaches; that I never have enough books or desks; that I yell and scream and care all the damn time, and still there's so much that's out of my control. . . ."

I stopped for air. They stared at me.

"Oh yeah, and that stunt Michelle Pfeifer pulls, where she goes to the kid's house in the dangerous gang neighborhood? And then later he comes over to her house and stays in her bedroom with her all night, talking about life? Totally illegal," I added.

They continued to stare.

———————

Popular media is inundated with the myth of the "hero teacher" who charges headfirst into troubled inner-city schools like a firefighter to an inferno, bearing the student victims to safety through a combination of charisma and innate righteousness. The students are then "saved" by the teacher's idealism, empathy, and willingness to put faith in kids who have been given up on by society as a whole.

This is not that type of book.

The other familiar model of teacher stories, perhaps best exemplified by educational activist and writer Jonathan Kozol, is the "teacher as a sociologist" theory, wherein schools and the profession of teaching are used as a lens through which to view socioeconomic inequity in the United States.

While I have learned a great deal from Kozol's writing, and though the following stories are in many ways about the day-to-day experiences of poor kids, ultimately this is not that type of book, either.

This book isn't a scathing indictment of inner-city education or even a story of disillusionment. It's a story about a suburban kid having her eyes opened and learning to distinguish between mitigated failure and qualified success. This is a book about being a new teacher: about the trial by fire that all teachers must undergo, about making mistakes, and about learning from one's own students. It's is a book about trying to work within a broken system, while at the same time being bolstered by the very same kids you came in wanting to save.

Introduction

How Many Lives Did Your Last Spreadsheet Change?

Eric Evans wasn't doing his work.

I had just given the twelfth-graders in my summer school class a writing assignment: "Have you ever done something that you regretted, or that made you feel guilty long afterwards? Discuss." We were reading John Knowles's *A Separate Peace*, and I kept thinking that if ever there were a book more disconnected from my inner-city students' lives than this tale of overprivileged youth at a thinly veiled fictionalization of Phillips Exeter, I had yet to see it. Or was it so disconnected? Couldn't themes of loss and guilt be relevant to even the most jaded, world-weary teens?

I hoped maybe they could. Otherwise, my lesson would be shot to hell.

But looking over at Eric, I knew I was in trouble. His paper was blank and his pen lay on his desk untouched. He was making exaggerated yawning and stretching noises, reclining his seat back against the lockers in the rear of the classroom. His classmates, looking up from their own work, had already noticed that he was not doing the assignment. I knew that in a moment his influence would cause me to lose my hold over them as well.

I came over to him. "Come on, Eric," I said. "Just try—don't you have anything you want to write about?"

"Miss Garon," he said, grinning at me slyly, "I'm a tough inner-city kid. Are you going to 'reach me,' or what?"

———

Explorers High School stands four stories tall, all Cold War–era architecture with no adornment or decoration to define what is otherwise a plain, square pile of faded red bricks. There are rusting "fall-out shelter" signs on some sides of the building and bars on the windows. Generations of students have remarked, not incorrectly, that the place looks like a prison.

Explorers is flanked on two sides by housing projects, and on a third side by the gated, incongruously plantation-style campus of a school for the deaf. From seven to ten every morning, a metal detector and a scanner are placed at each of the school's four main entrances, along with a slew of security guards with walkie-talkies. On particularly slow days, the gender-separated lines for "scanning" stretch around the corners of the school.

For my first four years and a summer, I took the 2 train from the Ninety-Sixth Street station in Manhattan all the way up to the northeast Bronx to get to Explorers. The trip lasted close to an hour door to door, and that was on a good day, when the train didn't become stuck (as it did, all too often) for twenty minutes in between 149th Street Grand Concourse and Third Avenue. On those days, I would find myself sprinting the half-mile from the subway station to the school, my backpack thumping against my back. If I were late enough, I'd figure "What the hell?" and stop to buy a sixty-cent coffee at one of the *bodegas* along the way. Then I would come up the steps to the school, past the metal detectors and the line of students who looked as though they were at the airport, patiently holding the belts and sneakers that they had taken off to speed up the scanning process.

———

It was an ad on a subway train that first gave me the idea to become a teacher. In March of 2003, my senior year of college, I was riding along listening to my MP3 player when I looked up and saw an advertisement for New York City Teaching Fellows—a black background with stark white lettering: "How many lives did your last spreadsheet change?"

The Teaching Fellows program seemed like a good deal. It would pay for me to get a master's degree in education (I only later found out that due to budget cuts relating to the Iraq war I would have to pony up half the cash); I would receive a full teacher's salary; and I would get to teach in a tough school where I could "make a difference."

The job seemed like a challenge, and that was what I was looking for. I liked kids—all my token transcript-building projects in high school and college had involved tutoring students in my upper-middle–class suburban community in everything from swimming to *bar mitzvah* preparation to arts and crafts. At Barnard, I had majored in English and psychology. I even had a couple years of counseling experience on a university crisis and suicide hotline; I thought this might prove useful working with high-needs kids, who I imagined would have a slew of emotional problems they would want to discuss with me during cozy heart-to-hearts after class.

Plus, my college graduation was two months away and I had no other plans.

I applied to the Fellows program, hoping to be assigned to teach high school English. I had spent so much time dawdling that by the time I heard that I had been granted an interview, in early May, the last round of the application process was drawing to a close. The program was trying to fill all its available spots as soon as possible. I had to prepare a demonstration lesson for the interview. I "taught" my favorite Wordsworth poem, "My Heart Leaps Up." I had always liked the line "The child is father of the man"—it seemed somehow appropriate for someone embarking on a career working with children. I ran over the allotted five minutes, got flustered, and started rambling about a hypothetical quiz that I would give were I teaching a real course instead of a mock lesson. Afterward I sat down, red-faced with embarrassment. I didn't feel that I had done very well. But due to the sheer force of my enthusiasm for Wordsworth, or more likely out of the hiring committee's desperation to fill the staggering number of teacher vacancies in the system, I was accepted to the Teaching Fellows program two days after my twenty-second birthday.

———

I interviewed at Explorers, a public high school of 4,700 students, at the beginning of our summer training. Due to subway block-ups, I arrived half an hour late for my interview. I ran into the English department office, which contained a small anteroom, at the end of which the assistant principal sat behind a Plexiglas wall. Of course, I was flustered and apologizing left and right. But the head of the English department seemed too immersed in the charts on his computer screen to care. He swiveled his chair toward me, asking in an almost bored tone of voice, "So, what are your views on education?"

I am not certain what he expected me to say, since I was fresh out of college and had never officially taught anything. But whatever I told him must have been what he wanted to hear. "Well," he said, after a few minutes, "the principal of the school is out today, but I'd basically like to 'sign you' now."

"Sign you"—it sounded like I was a basketball star. "Can I think about it for a couple of days?" I asked.

"Well, I don't think that's a very good idea, because we're trying to fill our spots pretty quickly so that we don't run short. You probably won't have a position if you wait much longer. . . ."

I was flattered that someone was so interested in hiring me that they'd push me into a contract on the spot. I signed.

———

Teaching Fellows summer training involved a combination of classes, observations, and supervised student teaching. Mrs. Walker, my cooperating teacher, was in her last summer before retirement. She was about five feet, five inches tall and slender, with smooth, almost black skin and a seemingly infinite wardrobe of elegant summer dresses. She couldn't have been older than fifty, but her approach to education was traditional, tough-love. "Everyone's too concerned with making things *fun* for them," she said, with just a trace of a Haitian accent in her otherwise impeccable English. She pronounced the word "fun" as though she'd been forced to swallow detergent. "And that's stupid— they just need to sit still and do the work, whether they like it or not!"

Mrs. Walker cut an imposing figure, despite her small size. Looking back, I admire her ferocity. She was a tough grader. Very tough. During my first week assisting her that summer, one of the brightest students in the class got a 72 on a test. "Miss, a 72? Why'd I get that?" Then he paused and said, "Wait . . . but that's good, coming from you, isn't it? Never mind." He sat down, looking defeated.

Another time, a student didn't answer when I took attendance because he wasn't paying attention. "Just mark him absent," Mrs. Walker snorted. Then later she said, "Did you mark him absent? Good!" The student was sitting *right there*. Her teaching methods motivated the students to write, in an essay on the theme of responsibility in John Knowles's *A Separate Peace*, that the character Gene should be forced to sit through Mrs. Walker's English class as a punishment for pushing his best friend Phinneas out of a tree. I laughed out loud when I read that, and then exhorted them to hurry and write something else before Mrs. Walker caught on.

The summer school class contained incoming and repeating twelfth-graders. Some were nearly my age, having missed years of school due to pregnancy, immigration, multiple academic failures, or parental illness. Most were only a few credits shy of graduating. They needed this class badly enough to come to an un-air-conditioned, graffiti-tagged classroom with undersized, wobbly desks. When the windows were open, which they had to be in June and July, they let in the smell of garbage rotting in the heat of the Bronx summer.

"Why are you guys here?" I asked on the first day Mrs. Walker let me teach a lesson on my own. I was hoping to inspire some revelation about the value of education and perseverance.

"Because second-period English was too early," said one of the football players whose knees stretched out three feet in front of him. Scattered giggles came from the back of the classroom.

A pudgy kid by the name of William Williams, whose hair was in neat cornrows, lifted his head up from the desk and said, "Like my momma said—'cause I fucked up." Then he put his head back down on the desk.

That's one way of putting it, I thought. But I said to the kids, "Can anyone tell me what makes the people sitting here in summer school different from their peers, who also flunked English, but are hanging around on the block instead?"

"We're stupider?" one girl replied.

This line of questioning wasn't going where I had intended.

"Has anyone read any good books lately?" I asked.

They all cracked up laughing.

"Okay, magazines?"

"You mean over the summer?"

"Yeah, now."

A small, shy girl named Hazel, with light brown ringlets and delicate bone structure, raised her hand. "Miss, I read a book," she said tentatively.

"Great! What was it about?"

"Well, it's about how not to get pregnant, and how to deal with smooth players who have lots of money."

"That sounds informative. Anyone else?"

"I read *Sports Illustrated*," offered a tall, amiable-looking kid named Alcides, sitting near the front.

No other students raised their hands.

"Well, okay, what do you guys do in the afternoons, when you go home?" I asked.

One of the students in the back, a hulking boy named Igor who had a perpetual grimace (and, I would later learn, was the head of the local Albanian gang) deadpanned, "I smoke a fat blunt."

The students around him laughed. I stared, disbelieving.

I told them to take out a piece of paper and write a paragraph explaining their motivation for coming to summer school. "Motivation is why you'd want to do something," I told them.

"Miss?"

"Yes, what's your name?"

"Kevin."

"Yes, Kevin?"

"I can't concentrate."

"Why?"

"Because I keep lookin' at your pretty face, Miss."

I blushed, and muttered, "Come on, Kevin, do you work." It had not escaped any of these kids that I was only a couple of years older than they were.

————

"Okay, this poem by Robert Frost . . . what's it about?" I asked them a couple of weeks later. I was teaching "Nothing Gold Can Stay," an eight-line poem about the impermanence of beauty. There was no response.

"Guys?" I tried again. Still nothing. They were all sleeping, doodling, or staring out the window. It was Monday. They'd obviously had a long weekend.

So I did what Mrs. Walker always did in these situations—told them to take out a piece of paper and write an essay. Eric Evans, a tall black kid who would take his contraband do-rag off whenever his unfailingly accurate sixth sense told him that the deans were approaching the classroom, but would put it back the moment they left, wrote one long, graphic sex scene. "I touched my girlfriend's ebony body in ecstasy, she moaned in ecstasy . . ." it read.

"Very interesting piece of creative writing," I scrawled in red pen at the top of his paper, "But I'm unclear on its relevance to the theme of 'Nothing Gold Can Stay.'"

The next day I returned the papers. A minute later, Eric called me over. "What does this mean?" he asked, pointing to my comments.

"It means I didn't understand how your essay has anything to do with the poem," I told him. "You talk about sex with your girlfriend for one and a half pages, and then you just tack on a random line from the poem at the end."

"Miss." He grinned slyly. "You *know* what I mean."

I did not, but it didn't seem wise to press for further explanation.

Later, when we read "The Road Not Taken," I explained about Frost's message of sometimes having to make the more difficult or less popular choices. "The 'road not taken' is the decision fewer people make, guys," I said. "Do you know what that's like?"

Eric raised his hand. "Miss, could this poem be about a woman?"

I misunderstood him. "You mean, could it apply to a woman as well?"

"Yeah."

"Well yeah, sure. Women also have to make difficult choices. . . ." I stopped and look at him, confused.

"No, I mean, the poem is about women. You choose the one not 'taken' . . . and that makes all the difference," he said. The class laughed, saying, "Ohhh, yeah."

Sexual interpretations of the poems became rampant. Listening to them, one might think that Robert Frost had written an entire anthology of erotic poetry—"Stopping by the Woods on a Snowy Evening," for instance, was met with enthusiastic discussion about the "gay horse" that is trying to figure out its sexual preferences.

"What?" I asked, bewildered by a reference that seemed to come out of nowhere.

William Williams appraised me with sympathy. "You know, 'My little horse must think it's queer. . . .' He hasn't decided if he's a fag or not, Miss."

A chorus of "Yeah, this poem is mad gay," resounded throughout the room.

I opted not to miss out on what we call, in education, the "teachable moment."

"Okay, first of all, when we're reading about something that you guys think is 'gay,' I want you to say it has 'homosexual undertones.' Can you say that?"

"Homosexual under . . . what?" they said, almost in unison.

"Undertones."

"So this poem has homosexual undertones?"

"Yeah . . . well, no, not really, but . . . well, I guess that's one interpretation."

When I wasn't in Mrs. Walker's English class, I was attending FA, or "Fellows Advisory," a special class taught by an experienced teacher wherein all the new fellows were supposed to learn lesson planning and classroom management skills. What it ended up being was more akin to group counseling. We, the new teachers, would all sit around bemoaning the injustices of our respective summer school programs.

"My students don't have any books!" one teacher would cry.

"You think that's bad? We have kids sitting on the windowsill because there aren't enough desks!" another would yell.

"Yeah, well our kids have to take the exact same English class two periods in a row, because they failed both English 7 and 8, but the school can't be bothered to create two different level summer school classes! These children aren't learning!"

"Why do you always call them 'these children,' like they're some sort of aliens? You have to get over your latent racism!"

It would go on like this until the lead teacher would call us to order, causing us to shift our focus toward lesson planning instead of complaining—much in the manner of our own students—about our schools, our fellow teachers, or our classes.

I remain profoundly grateful to those first summer school students who, having been granted a young and inexperienced summer school teacher, didn't use the opportunity to make my life a living hell. They sometimes slacked off, but they were never rude or disrespectful to this wide-eyed suburban kid from Virginia. I knew other teachers in the Fellows program who dropped out before completing summer school, citing horrific working conditions. One teacher I knew had his classroom set on fire. Thankfully, I never experienced anything like that.

————

Months after summer school ended, when I was well into my first year of teaching, a handsome young man flagged me down a couple of blocks from the school building. He was about a foot taller than I was, and sported a shiny pair of wire-rimmed glasses. Because of this, it took me a moment to recognize him.

"Miss Garon! Don't you remember me?" he asked.

"Eric Evans!" I sputtered, as everything zoomed into focus. "How are you? What are you up to these days?"

He gave me the rundown: Mrs. Walker had passed him with a 65—one of her more generous acts, I couldn't help thinking, since he'd done none of the work as far as I could tell—and so he was done with high school. Now he was living with his mom and working at McDonald's. He was thinking of enrolling in community college.

"You're smart! You should do it!"

He burst out laughing.

"Eric, what's so funny?"

"Miss, you're always, like, mad happy," he told me.

"Is that bad?"

"No, at first we thought it was annoying, but now . . . " he paused. "I don't know. We like it. You just gotta learn to be more strict—otherwise, those little punk-ass freshmen will be walkin' all over you."

He was right, of course. Despite my best efforts to fashion myself as a disciplinarian, the punk-ass freshmen were eating me for lunch.

"So, you're saying I should be . . . like . . . meaner?" I asked him, resisting the temptation to whip out a pen and take notes.

He furrowed his brow. "Nah, not really *meaner* . . . just . . . 'do *you*,' Miss. Don't front. Do you." He said this with finality.

I nodded. He gave me a hug and continued on his way. I didn't see him again after that.

Looking back, I realize he was giving me good advice. However, it took several years before I trusted myself enough, both as a teacher and a person, to know that he was right.

YEAR 1

Welcome to Ms. Garon's English Class!

A few rules for everyone's safety and enjoyment (and 5 points homework credit if you bring this back, signed by a parent):

1. No sucking candies, lollypops, gum, potato chips, Chinese take-out, Doritos, seed packets, or any other snack/food substances are allowed in this class. To that end, there will be no strolling back and forth from the trash can, either. All wrappers and lollypop sticks will be thrown away before entering the classroom. Drinks in a bottle are allowed, as long as they are kept in their containers and do not cause a mess or a disturbance.

2. Anyone who shoots garbage at the trash can and misses has to clean up the whole room after class.

3. Any video games, walk-men, MP3 players, or other devices with or without headphones will be confiscated if I see them, and may or may not be given back. They are to remain in your jacket, pocket, backpack, whatever. Just do not allow them to be visible. Yes, I see those headphones underneath your hood. Do you really think Ms. Garon is blind?

4. You are to come prepared for class. This means bringing paper, a marble notebook, pens or pencils, any books or packets we are reading, a homework folder, and of course your homework. You will be docked points for being unprepared. Enough said.

5. Ms. Garon comes to class before the bell, and so should you. Lateness will result in a deduction (that means you lose those points) from your class participation grade. School is your "job." You need to be here on time. No, I do not care that the line was long at the metal detectors. Wake up earlier. Take a Pop Tart to go. Become friends with the bus driver or the security guards.

6. If you do not come to class, you will be marked absent. You can only make up work if your absence is excused, meaning that a

parent/guardian, doctor, lawyer, judge, or someone else important writes me a note vouching for your whereabouts. Yes, I can always detect forgeries. I am mad smart that way.

7. You know all those rules about raising your hand when you want to speak, staying in your assigned seat unless the teacher gives you permission to move around, being respectful to your peers and your teacher, and behaving maturely? Yeah, those same rules apply in here, too.

8. Your grade will be computed in the following manner:
    -   30% class participation (attendance, coming on time, acting alert).
    -   30% homework and class work (Ms. Garon only takes late work if you have an excused absence).
    -   40% tests, quizzes, and special projects (which you can only make up with an excused absence note!).

9. No coming to class stoned.

I have read and understand these rules.

_____   _____
student's signature   student ID #

_____   _____
parent/guardian's signature   parent/guardian phone #

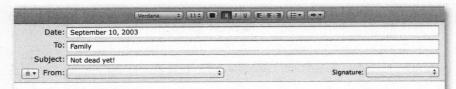

Date: September 10, 2003
To: Family
Subject: Not dead yet!
From: Signature:

I'm two days into teaching high school English, and I'm still alive. Aside from inappropriate attention and love notes from members of the opposite sex (and I mean from the faculty, not the students), my difficulties have been manifold, including: not having *any* books for my kids, failing copy machines, classrooms that are assigned to my ninth-grade English class and a tenth-grade social studies class for the same period, having to substitute in a tenth-grade science class for which I wasn't left a lesson plan or an attendance form, having a nonfunctional key to the teachers' ladies room (I have to stand outside and wait for someone else to let me in), and being observed by some official from the Board of Education on my second day teaching to see if I was implementing some new literacy program for which I haven't been trained despite the state mandate that I go to this training. (The school wanted to send me, but it cost $5K. They didn't have $5K.)

My kids are great. Yesterday and today, I had them write me "Dear Ms. Garon" letters introducing themselves. Here are some of my favorite sections (exact spelling included):

"The movie that best describe how I feel is The Fast and The Ferious. *I love speed, danger, and risks. My favorite car is a Honda Civic with a big wing in the back. Speed describes the way I live."*

"I love softball that's pretty much all I have to tell you . . . other than I have had an opperation for my appendics which I really think you did not want to know that but that's my only medical problem well I guess not anymore since it's out of my stomach. Oh yes I do have another medical problem well I have something with my kidney so I get pains sometimes but I haven't got any pain in a while so you don't need to worry that's all you need to know."

"I would like you to know that sometimes I have a problem with reading out loud. But I can read good in my mind. Oh and you will have to repeat the homework because sometimes I don't write it down. Oh and I didn't see the movie Freddy vs. Jason *but I've heard it was hot."*

"I can't write good for nothing. I like video games, art, and being lay-z. I can draw really good but not as good as I would like to draw. So I don't really show my pics off. My life is a little weird because I live with my mom and my mom lives with the landlord because he's her boyfriend but the boyfriend's X had no place to stay so she lives with us also and the boyfriend's X has a little girl because it's the boyfriend's kid and the kid is with him because he does not pay child support. Anyway here's everyone who lives in my house: Me, my mom, broter, sester, dog, step-dad, step-dad's X, a tertule. We had two tertules but one just disaperd. So that's just liveing with my mom . . . my dad is a hole nother story. PS -- I can't write good becuase I'm left handed."

"How are you doing? I'm fine just chillin'. Today is the 2nd day of school and it's aight, I've seen mad chicks its a wrap this year. My summer was mad wak, I'm hoping this winter is going to be poppin'. Really I have nothing else to say."

My ninth-graders try to be bad-asses, but they just aren't convincing. For starters, they're very small; they came in yesterday complaining that the big kids were pushing them around in the hallway. And they're so clearly still kids that you can't help thinking they're cute. Yesterday afternoon several of them ran up to me in the hallway (I'm their homeroom teacher) all flustered and upset because they didn't understand their schedules for the next morning. Once I pointed them in the right direction, they resumed their usual swagger, pants hanging down, boxers exposed, contraband do-rags on heads.

All for now—must plan lessons.

Date: September 15, 2003

To: Family

Subject: Everything you ever wanted to know about prison . . .

From: Signature:

On Friday, I stashed my students' books in a locker in the classroom. I came in Monday to get the books, only to find that the combination lock will not open. I tried a million times, to no avail. The students came in to find me banging my head against the locker, frustrated because my entire lesson plan was dependent upon these books. The students all said, "Miss, let me try!" They all tried. No one succeeded.

I decided we needed to get down to business as best we could. This was a double period class (although we'd wasted some of our time trying to get the damn books out of the locker), so I still had over an hour and no materials. The book we were supposed to be reading is about a teenager who went to prison, so I said, "Okay, who has impressions of prison that they'd like to share?" All the hands went up, but the main thing everyone wanted to say was that you shouldn't drop the soap in the shower. Very original. They all cracked up laughing.

I invented a makeshift lesson about prison (a topic about which I know next to nothing), asking the kids to brainstorm about impressions of prison based on movies, personal experience, books, etc. We talked about how it might feel to be in prison as a young teenager. We talked about getting beaten up, eating bad food, and of course being raped in the shower (which seemed to be a subject of serious interest to them). Students shared their own experiences of having family members who had been to prison.

Midway through the class, half my students who I had thought were absent wandered in. Turns out they'd just come from some meeting with the head discipline guy, and they'd all been suspended for a few days. Terrific. (Naturally, they had no idea why.)

With five minutes left in the period, I ran out of prison-related things to talk about, so I told the kids to just chill out. Meanwhile, I went to work on the locker again. One of my students said, "Hey, Miss, there's a sticker in the back!" We looked at the sticker. It turns out I'd remembered the combination wrong. The bell rang just then. Go figure.

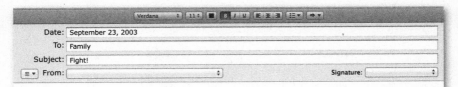

So, the bell rings after ninth period, and I allow my students to go out for a water break since I have them for tenth period as well. The door to the classroom is open, and I'm sorting papers when I hear two voices yelling at each other. A crowd forms around them like magnets—where did all these kids *come from?*—and then there's the unmistakable noise that indicates someone has just thrown a punch: the hallway *roars.* It sounds like a bomb going off. Everyone starts screaming, the crowd of about one hundred kids (and more streaming in every second) starts stomping and yelling . . . all hell breaks loose. All of this takes place in a matter of seconds.

My room is right next to the social studies office. The assistant principal of social studies is a friendly man named Mr. Gjoni; sometimes he and I chat between classes. Now we both sprint down the hall, straight into the throng. We're not supposed to break up fights (our teacher's health care doesn't cover injuries we might sustain), but Mr. Gjoni goes right at the fighters and starts pulling them apart. Meanwhile, I spread my arms as wide as I can and push all the spectators against the wall to make sure they don't get caught in the crossfire (we're supposed to do this in case someone whips out a weapon or something), and to clear a path for the security guards, who come running in about ten seconds later.

One of the "suspects" sprints through the crowd I've just cleared and down the hall. A couple of security guards turn and follow in hot pursuit. Pandemonium continues to ensue, with kids yelling and screaming and all clamoring to give their version of what happened.

After about two minutes, the floor is swarming with administrators and school safety officers, and everyone is yelling for the kids to go back to class. My students race into the room because they all want to talk about what happened, except for two girls who beg to be let out again because they never managed to get through the hallway to the bathroom. I figure we won't get anything done until we debrief, so everyone talks about the fight for five minutes, and then we get back to our work.

CHAPTER 1

Carlos

The student I remember best from my first semester of teaching is Carlos. A freshman, he was nearly sixteen, and a handsome kid—five feet, eight inches with close-cropped, black, curly hair, dark skin, and luminous, almost black eyes. He was added to the roster of my English class about two weeks into the school year. For the first month or so that I knew him, he never said a word; I took his silence for lack of interest and wrote him off as a slacker. Then we read Walter Dean Myers's *Monster*, a book about a teenager on trial for murder, and Carlos approached me at my desk after class. He waited patiently for the other students to leave.

"Miss," he whispered, "I like this book."

"I'm so glad to hear that, Carlos," I said. I was suspicious—my experience with summer school made me wonder if I was being set up.

"It's kind of similar to my life."

"Really?"

"Yeah, I did some time in 'juvey' a while back. . . ." Carlos paused, seeming surprised at his own revelation. "I was doing drugs, stealing . . . I got in trouble, Miss. Doing time in juvey made me think a lot about my life."

His honesty and reflective attitude surprised me. With the stunning discernment of someone who has been teaching for exactly three months, I concluded that this was the single most self-aware ninth-grader I would ever meet—and here he was, coming to *me* for guidance. All my teaching experience to date had clearly been preparing me for this point.

"Carlos," I said, "you're missing a few reading responses. If you write me a page or two about how this book relates to your experiences, we could call it even."

"You'd let me do that?"

"Absolutely."

The next day, Carlos turned in a beautifully written piece about his experiences in juvenile detention center, his time on the street selling drugs, and the ways in which he wished to improve his life. The kid had a flare for writing; that much was clear to me. Moreover, I started to see him in a different light. He rarely raised his hand in class, but his eyes flickered with attention and intelligence, and I realized that, slacker or not, he wasn't missing a beat. He would often come to speak to me after class about everything from his life, to the reading, to other students. "Miss, Chantal's havin' some problems with her man . . ." he would say. "I been talking to her about it."

The girls would turn to Carlos for advice about their love lives, knowing that he was savvy enough to give good strategic advice, but sensitive enough to provide a listening ear. I would see him with his arms around girls in the hallway, almost paternally, as they cried into his shoulder.

One morning in October, two deans burst into our classroom. "Obed Gonzalez," they announced. "You're coming with us. Get your stuff." I would later realize these kinds of sudden and unapologetic interruptions were routine, but in my first few months they were still shocking.

Obed, the kid in question, was a sweetheart; a talented math student (his teacher told me he made all A's), he had never given me any problems. He looked surprised, but was cooperative. He gathered his books and coat into his bag.

"Could you please tell me what's going on?" I asked the deans. "Is Obed in trouble?"

"Probably," one of them replied in that same monotone as he slammed the door to my classroom behind him. Obed cast a forlorn look at me through the glass window of our door before he was escorted out of sight.

The moment the bell rang, Carlos was at my desk.

"I have to talk to you about Obed," he said.

"About Obed? Do you know what's up?"

"Yeah . . . I know why they took him out."

"You do?"

"This guy pulled a knife on us yesterday outside art class."

I gasped. "No!"

In response, Carlos shot me an exasperated look that I understood to mean something like this: *Oh, for crying out loud, Miss, you know this type of thing happens around here. Pull yourself together, okay?*

"So how was Obed involved?" I tried to sound neutral.

"Well . . . with Obed, it was all self-defense," Carlos said. I was not sure what he meant by that.

Then he looked away and said, "Miss, here's the problem: If my parents find out about this, that I got in a 'situation' in school, even if it's not my fault, they gonna take me out of this school . . . and I want to stay here."

He could get out of here? In a way, I wanted to call his parents right then and tell them, "Get Carlos to another school! He's smart! He has so much promise!" Despite the fact that I had already met a slew of nice kids who were equally smart and promising, on a gut level I was still laboring under a certain misapprehension: that my role as an inner-city school teacher was, among other things, to identify "good" kids who didn't belong in a school like this one and to get them out.

Then I caught myself. If his parents could afford better, Carlos would already be there, I reasoned. And short of testing into one of the magnet programs—a herculean feat for any kid, let alone one coming from a non-English speaking background—there weren't many other options. The other public high schools in the area were no "better" than this one.

I returned to Carlos, who appraised me, waiting for an answer. "Carlos, you realize, if this comes to be an issue, you may need to speak out on Obed's behalf, to say it was self-defense—even if it means leaving this school."

He sighed. "I know Miss. Obed and I are mad tight. I'll do that for him, you know? But . . ." Then he bit his lip and said, "Yeah, Miss, you're right . . . I'll come with you to talk to the deans."

We went downstairs to the basement security offices. I barged in, expecting to argue. Lo and behold, there was Obed, but not in trouble— rather, he sat in a swivel chair leafing through a notebook of what appeared to be student mug shots. "Oh, hey Miss! Hi Carlos!" he called cheerfully.

"Carlos? As in, Carlos de la Cruz?" the security guard asked, over-hearing.

"Yo, I'm Carlos."

"Ah, so you saw what happened. We have to take a statement from you."

Carlos looked at me with a note of pleading in his eyes.

"Sir?" I asked. "Do you think we might be able to keep Carlos's parents out of this? He'd kind of like to stay here, and his parents have threatened to remove him from school if he is involved in any violent situations . . ." I trailed off. I was embarrassed, but I wasn't sure in front of whom: the security guard, to whom this request no doubt sounded childishly impractical? Or Carlos, who was counting on me for more than this weak stand?

"No can do, we're mandated to alert the parents," the security guard said with finality.

"Sorry, Carlos," I whispered.

"It's okay, Miss," he muttered bitterly. "It's not your fault this school is wack."

————

But as it turned out, Carlos stayed in our school, and I didn't hear from his parents one way or another. At one point I called them at home. I knew, from what Carlos had told me, that they spoke very little English; I managed to convey to them that their son was making excellent progress in my class, and they seemed bemused that I would bother to call them for this reason alone.

When I asked Carlos about this, he told me, "They really only care if I'm in trouble or whatever, Miss."

"Do you want to tell me about that?"

"I just feel like they don't care about me, you know? Like, I can't talk to them about nothing."

"I'm sorry. That must be lonely."

"Yeah . . . we don't really get along right now anyway."

In truth, Carlos's relationship with his parents sounded typical of any teenager—I could see myself having said the same thing at age sixteen. Perhaps it was this knowledge that we weren't actually so different that endeared Carlos to me. Or perhaps it was just his nature I found appealing—that he managed to be wise and brave, but still a little bit fragile. I wanted to nurture him, to not let him slip.

I made a mental note to check on him regularly. This turned out to be easy, since he often came to me after class to talk about his various "problems," most of which were romantic in nature. I relished these conversations and the opportunity they provided for me to get to know Carlos; at the same time, I felt nervous that we would be misunderstood. A handsome, lovelorn student in search of guidance, a very young female teacher, still insecure about her role in the classroom . . . there were infinite potential pitfalls. I was always careful to leave the classroom door wide open, so that anyone could poke their heads in to see that nothing illicit was going on between us.

One morning, Carlos came into class looking pale and sweaty, with red-rimmed eyes. He went straight to his desk—without saying hi, I noted—and put his head down. He didn't look up for the rest of the period. I decided not to say anything until class ended. When the bell rang and all the students left, he stayed. So I went to where he was sitting, still with his head on the desk, and said, "Hey kiddo, what's going on?"

He looked up at me. His eyes were bloodshot. "Miss, I'm drunk," he said, pressing his thumb and index finger against his sinuses and closing his eyes.

This was hardly news. Sitting three feet away, I could smell the alcohol emanating from his pores.

"Yes, I've noticed. You wanna tell me how that happened?"

"Well, so you know how I'm on the late schedule?"

Due to overcrowding, our school had two "schedules"—early and late. Eleventh- and twelfth-graders were on the early schedule; they had class from 7 a.m. until roughly 12:15 p.m. At the 12:15 bell they left the building, whereupon the ninth- and tenth-graders had their late schedule classes from 12:30 to 5:45 p.m. At that hour it was dark, leaving the youngsters to walk home in poorly lit gang territory. This would have worried me more if the kids had been inclined to stay that long, but most of them weren't—they tended to leave school around 3:45 p.m. when their friends were let out of neighboring high schools, cutting their last two or even three classes on a daily basis.

In the midst of my worries about their absence at the late afternoon, I had not even considered that the kids could get into trouble in the morning, between the time their parents left for work, and noon, when they started lining up at the front doors of the school for scanning. Now, Carlos was telling me that there had been a substantial amount of drinking going on during the unsupervised hours.

"So no one's home where you guys are drinking?"

"Nope."

"And this has happened before?"

"Uh-huh . . . but I usually don't get like this."

"Why the hell would you be drinking at all before school, Carlos? You're smarter than that!"

"I don't know, Miss. There were all these people, and I don't want to seem weak."

It shouldn't have been surprising to me that he had caved to peer pressure. For all Carlos's maturity, he was still subject to the same laws that governed all sixteen-year-old boys. Yet, the fact that he was a normal teenager was somehow disappointing to me.

There is only one adult here, I reminded myself.

"Okay. Have you eaten anything all day?"

"Um . . . I had a piece of bread for breakfast?"

"Not good enough. No wonder the alcohol hit you so hard." I went to my pantry closet and pulled out some graham crackers and a jar of Skippy peanut butter that were left over from a class party I had thrown a while ago. Carlos protested—"No. Miss, I'm fine! You don't need to do this."

Ignoring him, I spread some peanut butter on a cracker with a plastic spoon, and placed it in front of him on a paper towel. "Here. Eat up."

He started to eat, slowly at first, but then devoured the peanut butter and graham crackers. I made him another sandwich. Then I took a large plastic party cup to the water fountain in the hallway and filled the cup to the brim. *Thank god I don't have a class right now*, I thought to myself. I returned to the room, closing the door behind me.

"You're going to drink this entire thing, mister."

"Miss . . ." He groaned, and put his head in his hands.

"Drink it, Carlos. Being drunk, or hungover—whatever you are at this point—it's basically a very bad case of dehydration. I'm going to sit here, and you need to drink all this water."

He seemed to think about it for a moment, and then resign himself to the idea that it wouldn't do any good to argue. He downed the water. I watched, wondering if it made me a bad teacher that I hadn't turned him over to the deans on account of his extra-curricular activities.

"Now. You wanna tell me who was involved?"

"Um . . . nah. I'd feel bad."

I didn't pursue the issue; I told myself that he would be too loyal a friend to ever yield. This may have been true. Mostly, I was content to have made a half-hearted attempt to pursue this as a legitimate disciplinary issue, so that now I could go back to protecting him from the punishment he would have coming to him if I hadn't intervened.

"Okay," I said. "I'm letting you off the hook. But you need to promise me something. The next time they start drinking, especially before school—you are out of there, you hear me? Just leave. I don't care what else is going on."

"Yeah, I know, Miss. I'm sorry."

"Don't apologize to me! Just don't put yourself in this position again, okay?"

He looked down at the table and nodded once. I noticed he was fiddling with the empty cup.

"So. Do you need me to write you a late-pass to Art?"

"Nah. It's my fault. I'll just take the rap—she can't do nothing to me anyway 'cause I'm there most of the time."

He got up and wearily gathered his stuff. Sitting on my desk, I watched him. He swung his backpack over his shoulder and came over to the desk. When he reached out his closed fist for a "pound," I accepted; we had never greeted each other this way before, but now it seemed important somehow. *We're still pals.*

"I'll catch you later, Miss."

"Carlos."

"Yeah?"

He was standing in front of me. I reached up and took his little face in my hands, angling it slightly downwards towards me so that his eyes would meet mine.

"If you ever come to school drunk again, I will kick your ass from here 'til next Tuesday. Do we understand each other?"

He held my gaze and nodded. Then he smiled, though not in a conspiratorial "*I know you don't mean that*" kind of way—more in an understanding "*I am aware that you've just risked your teaching license for my ass*" kind of way.

He left the classroom. I watched him make his way down the hallway. There was a lump in my throat, though I couldn't have said exactly why.

Date: October 27, 2003
To: Family
Subject: Fight—again!
From: **Signature:**

In the four-minute period between dismissal from tenth period (my class) and the beginning of eleventh period, two of my students managed to fight so badly that they both ended up bleeding and with broken wrists/fingers. Good grief. One of the warriors, Nora, I reported as an abuse case last week. The other is one of my top students, "Lisa." The fight was over "Jeremy," Lisa's boyfriend. Apparently Nora has a thing for Jeremy, also. Lisa was standing around chatting with a group of kids, and suddenly Nora leaped upon her and started punching her from behind. Once Lisa got her bearings, the fight descended into hair pulling, scratching, beating, and all kinds of other brutality. It was relentless. Nora's face was bleeding, and I was worried they were going to claw each other's eyes out.

I'll preface the following by saying this: I *know* I'm not supposed to get involved. But I just couldn't stand to see them clawing each other like that. *"Go get security!"* I yelled to the ten or so kids who had not yet gone to their next class as I tried to pry the girls apart. (They are pretty small.) No one budged. It was as if I were speaking Greek or something. Meanwhile, a group of on-lookers pooled, mouths agape, at the doorway. None of them went to get security either. The girls were still throwing each other around, knocking desks over in the process, and no one was coming. *"Go get security!"* I yelled again, in desperation, as I tried to push them away from each other. Jeremy, the boy over whom they were fighting, started (slowly) out of the room to get security, and Carlos came to his senses and helped me separate the girls. He grabbed Nora off Lisa and walked her away, gently, with his arm around her to calm her down.

Just then the head of the UFT burst in, walkie-talkie in hand, and helped me get rid of all the extra kids who were milling around at the front of the room. I went downstairs to file a disciplinary report, and both girls were in the office receiving suspensions within the next two minutes, although I don't think they cared much.

Why did they have to fight like that, to turn from little girls into feral cats? I don't get it. . . . I'm close with this group of kids (they're my homeroom class), and so perhaps that's why I am so angry with them, and more than a little bit disappointed. There was something upsetting about seeing them be so vicious with one another.

CHAPTER TWO

Alex

In the early evenings, my students—Damien, Alex, Anthony, Desi, Matt—and I would huddle our desks together in the center of the classroom. We were in that last period of the day—fourteenth, ending at 5:55 p.m.—and the abysmal attendance (those kids were the only ones who ever showed up) was a testament to how poorly this schedule was working out.

There was something very odd, surreal even, about being in the school after dark. It seemed incongruous with my idea of what school was "like"—when I sat at home envisioning how my lessons would go with these kids, in my mind the sun was always streaming into a packed classroom. Months after I had been teaching fourteenth period, always the same five students, it still jarred me to look out the windows into the dark and see only the reflection of the flickering fluorescent ceiling lights.

The room was drafty, cavernous with just the six of us inside. The kids often wore their hats and gloves at their desks. Outside, the hallway was so empty that you could hear the echo of a person's footsteps long after he or she had passed by the door to our classroom. We left our door open, a silent encouragement to anyone who might be walking by and feel like stopping in. Sometimes, teachers who had had none of their students show up that period, or even sympathetic administrators, would enter and chat with us. We liked when that happened, especially if it was a cool young teacher, or even the deputy dean of security, who, unlike his supervisor, was easy-going and made good jokes: When one of the kids had said to him "You can't take away my hat—you're not my father!" He had responded, "Yeah? How do *you* know?" It relieved us from the unnerving sensation that we were the last people left in the building.

The kids in that class were freshmen repeaters. Privately, I called them Super-Freshmen. They were anywhere from sixteen to nineteen years old and were having their second or third go at freshman English. By comparison, I was twenty-two. Far from being the slackers I had been assured they would be (and that they definitely *were* in some of their other classes), they worked enthusiastically, taking it as a point of pride that out of the thirty-something kids on the roster, they were the only five who would pass. Once, we had an interloper for about a week—his name was Brian. He was on the roster, too. He showed up midsemester, hung out for a few days, and then vanished as inexplicably as he had first appeared. For months, the remaining kids hounded me to make sure that I would not pass him: "Yo Miss, Brian failed, right? How's he gonna show up for five days, and then think you gonna pass him? That's whack!" Brian had expressed no such belief, at least not to me—but the kids were endlessly cackling over his presumed audacity.

That fall, we were assigned to read *It Happened to Nancy*, which was essentially a cautionary pamphlet turned into a young adult novel. The book was written in faux-diary format, and the plot was simple: Nancy, an innocent white teenager from a suburban neighborhood in a fly-over state, meets a hot guy named Colin at a Bruce Springsteen concert. They strike up a relationship, and Colin tells Nancy that she reminds him of his younger sister, who is dead from some childhood illness. This revelation causes Nancy to fall in love with Colin. She invites Colin to her house, where he proceeds to drug her, rape her, and then vanish. Afterward, it turns out that Colin is actually in his thirties (not nineteen, like he told Nancy!) and a convicted child molester to boot. Also, he has

AIDS. The rest of the book chronicles Nancy's struggle with the disease and untimely death, much to the dismay of her unfailingly supportive, not to mention good-looking, group of friends.

My students pronounced *It Happened to Nancy* the most preposterous piece of trash they had ever read. For starters, we all thought it was unrealistic that someone succumbing to late-stage AIDS would be healthy enough to be riding a bicycle through the corn-fields in the sunset and then chronicle it all in a diary. But beyond that, I think they were indignant at the perceived condescension. No way would any of them have invited a total stranger into their homes, they assured me—"That's mad stupid! Miss, you *asking* to get raped and murdered if you do that! No offense, but white girls is whack!"

So, I went to the book closet to find a replacement. The pickings were slim. I brought them two books to choose from. The first, I can't remember. The second was John Knowles's *A Separate Peace*.

They went for John Knowles. I think it was because I said offhandedly, the day I brought in the two books to choose from, "This one might be too challenging." I had read it with the summer school students before them, with little success—but somehow, my Super-Freshmen took to it. I would sit on top of my desk, Indian-style, in the center of that overlarge, cold classroom and read aloud to them, ten to fifteen pages at a time. They would group their desks around mine in a little cluster and follow along. Then we would discuss it.

It was one of those days that I asked them, in line with the book's flashback narration (which, we all agreed, was more effective than some fake journal): "Where do you guys see yourselves in ten years?"

Damien, the oldest and my class clown, was the first to shoot his hand in the air. Before I could even call on him, he delivered his line: "I'm going to be a male prostitute!" The class burst out laughing. He pumped his fists in the air and grinned.

"Okay, okay," I said, rolling my eyes. "Someone else."

Desi looked bored—but that was just her way. She was our class's old soul—and the lone girl. At sixteen, she had already had one abortion three years prior; later that year, she would have a second. She had bulging eyes that were heavily lidded, reminding me of a black moor goldfish, but somehow this made her seem more perceptive.

"God, I just hope I'm out of high school," she said, flashing a quick smile. Murmurs of agreement came from the peanut gallery.

I looked at Alex. To me, he was the most intriguing of the five. He had a small, sculpted face, wire-rimmed glasses, and tiny cornrows. When we read anything complicated, he would wait until his peers all had their turns guessing at the meaning; then, he would raise his hand and illuminate everything. Though he was well-liked and recognized for being intelligent, he was never cocky. I would catch his eye across the room sometimes, and he would smile at me; we were in on something together, though I would have been hard-pressed to say exactly what.

I knew Alex was affiliated with a group of kids who dealt crack. When I confronted him at one point, he told me that this group could pull in $6,000 on a good day. Though he had decent attendance to my class that term, he explained to me that the opportunity cost of going to school *every* day was too much when that kind of money was involved. I had a hard time arguing.

Now he looked at me appraisingly. "Miss," he said, "I'm pretty sure by the time I'm thirty I'll either be in jail or dead."

There was a moment of dead silence, punctuated by my dropping the cap to the dry erase marker. One of the kids helped me retrieve it, and then I sat down on the desk and stared at Alex.

"Why does it have to be that way?" I said. Then, forgetting to address the entire group, I blurted out, "You're smart, Alex. You could do tons of things with your life, besides dealing. You have some control over this situation, you know. Couldn't things be different?"

Damien answered. He got up and sat on top of the desk next to me. "Miss, that's the world we live in," he said. His voice held no rudeness or sarcasm; if anything, it held sympathy. The other kids nodded, murmuring in assent.

We sat quietly. After a few moments, I looked up at Alex, and he gave me a smile of such understanding I could have kissed him.

When the bell rang, the kids pulled on their coats and donned gloves and hats if they weren't already wearing them. As they bundled up for their exit into the cold night, I wanted to hold on to them, to keep them safe here with me.

"C'mon, Miss. Smile," said Damien. They each hugged me and filed out the door, shoving each other playfully, arms over each other's shoulders. A picture of high school bliss, they seemed for that moment to be at ease in the world.

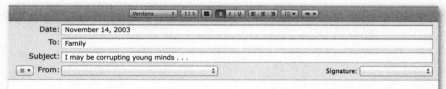

I've been reading this book *PUSH*, by Sapphire, with my ninth-grade repeaters. It's about a sixteen-year-old girl from the projects who, at the book's beginning, is pregnant with her second child by her father. Yeah, it's graphic and vulgar. It's also a well-written and thought-provoking narrative. The kids are into it.

I read the book to them aloud in class, and now they're doing projects related to it. They have the option of making a detailed poster to advertise the book, drawing a graphic rendition of it in comic book form (must be at least ten panels), writing an epilogue, or creating a journal from the point of view of a secondary character. They like this sort of thing because it gives them a chance to be artistic and creative (and some of them have a lot of talent).

Oddly, the Board of Ed encourages me to have my seventeen-year-olds spend whole periods drawing in crayon. . . . They call it "visualization." Whatever.

In my view, this is a reward to them for having done a lot of good assignments relating to this book. They were able to connect it with their lives in a lot of ways, and they surprised me with the honesty and high quality of their writing. I was proud of them.

However, one of the Special Education teachers feels that I'm corrupting their minds by letting them read this book due to its explicit content. "Am I giving you guys any ideas you haven't thought of? Any curses you've never heard?" I asked. They rolled their eyes and one girl (she's strong, brave, and really one of my favorites) said frankly, "Miss, I had an abortion when I was fourteen. Give it a rest." Point taken. I asked my assistant principal just to be on the safe side, and he pointed out that if the book is in the library (which it is) then I'm covered.

Date: December 23, 2003
To: Family
Subject: I should have thrown more parties in college.
From:
Signature:

I planned a party for my students because it's the day before Christmas Eve and only half of them are here, anyway, which makes it stupid to try and teach a lesson. Besides, it seems like all the other teachers are always giving their kids movies and parties, so I thought I would be nice for once. I made two special CDs titled "Miss Garon's Party Mix Volumes 1&2," which included all their favorite rap songs, with edited lyrics to get rid of the bad language. It also included the *South Park* version of "Oh Holy Night," and by their popular request, the Adam Sandler Hanukkah song. I brought in peanut butter, marshmallow fluff, and graham crackers so that they could have a snack, but not be too sugared up for their next class. (Giving them candy is a bad idea, I've learned.)

As it turns out, I'm an event-planning genius. The party was a huge hit . . . too much of a hit. Ninth period, other kids started coming in from other classes. At first, there were only one or two kids from my eighth-period class who had stayed over. Then more kids came. Someone wanted to go get more girls for dancing. A whole bunch of guys with do-rags walked in and sat in the corner, looking surly and intimidating. I did not know them.

I was getting a little nervous. I opened the door and asked a security guard, "Is this okay that they're all here?"

"Are they bugging you?" he asked.

"Well . . . no . . . not really. They're just sitting around dipping graham crackers in peanut butter."

"So that's fine then. Just call if you have a problem," he said.

The dean of security didn't agree. Ten minutes later he barged in and asked for the IDs of every single person who wasn't on my attendance roster. All the partygoers got their IDs confiscated, and now they have detention after the break.

I felt so bad. I figured I was doing everyone a favor by keeping the stray kids out of the hallway. Instead, I got a huge lecture from the dean about not allowing anyone into my class who isn't on the attendance roster. I was embarrassed. Definitely not a Christmas miracle, by any means.

The students were apologetic. "Why didn't you just 'take him out,' Miss?" they asked. Right, of course that's the logical solution—just beat up the dean.

They did help me clean up, though, after I instituted the "everyone pick up one piece of trash" rule. They also gave me gifts, including a Santa Claus mug filled with candy and a plaster casting of some angels praying. Perfect for a nice Jewish girl! It was sweet. As they were filing out the door, they all hugged me and said, "Thanks for being so nice," and that kind of made up for the dean coming in and yelling at me. Meanwhile, my assistant principal thought the whole incident was hilarious, particularly the part about the graham crackers, though I don't understand why.

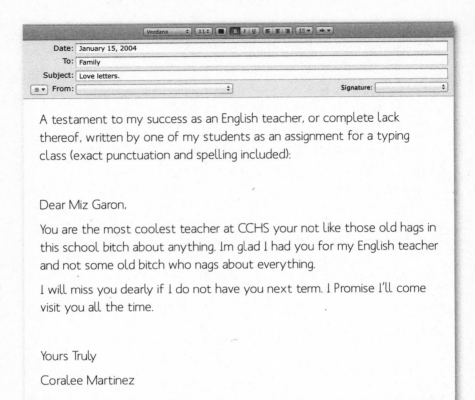

Date: January 15, 2004

To: Family

Subject: Love letters.

From: Signature:

A testament to my success as an English teacher, or complete lack thereof, written by one of my students as an assignment for a typing class (exact punctuation and spelling included):

Dear Miz Garon,

You are the most coolest teacher at CCHS your not like those old hags in this school bitch about anything. Im glad I had you for my English teacher and not some old bitch who nags about everything.

I will miss you dearly if I do not have you next term. I Promise I'll come visit you all the time.

Yours Truly

Coralee Martinez

Date: February 13, 2004
To: Family
Subject: My job is sometimes awesome.
From: Signature:

It's a week into the new semester. Today I had to preemptively break up a duel involving plastic utensils just before thirteenth period. (I figured everything would have been fine until someone got hurt, and then all hell would have broken loose.) Immediately afterwards, I had to bring my thirteenth-fourteenth period class down to the auditorium for an assembly on discipline and security, during which several of them managed to land themselves in detention for smarting off to the deans. I was embarrassed.

Upon returning to class, I had the kids read the poems of the Harlem Renaissance and discuss the relationships between black and white people during that time. Then we played the music of Tupac Shakur and Jay-Z (both rappers who talk a lot about the plight of African Americans in the ghetto) and discussed whether things have changed since the Harlem Renaissance era. The discussion was heated, and the students were enamored of the fact that they were allowed to listen to rap music in class.

I told the boys (our class is mostly male) that if they were good I would give them free reign over the boom box at the end of class. They turned on this song "Heya" by Outkast, which they all knew the words to, and started dancing around the classroom, singing along.

It was one of those moments wherein I realized why I do this: here I was in a school in the Bronx, surrounded by fifteen-year-old disciplinary nightmares who were leaping, dancing around me, singing at the tops of their lungs as I cleaned the classroom. These little men were jubilant, and it was only Thursday! One of the deans heard the commotion, looked in and said, "God, I wondered if they killed you!" and I said, "No, I allowed this," and she laughed and we looked on as they jumped and sang. Several of them came over and hugged me while simultaneously bouncing up and down and rapping. It was overwhelming, hilarious, and kind of adorable, and I was filled with this sensation of "How on earth did I get here?" but in the happiest way the thought could be phrased.

I feel lucky to have a job like this; it's exhausting, frustrating, and makes me worry to death sometimes, but it never gets boring, and is often inspiring.

CHAPTER THREE

Kayron

Here is one cardinal rule of being a teacher: You're not supposed to play favorites, let alone out-rightly dislike your students, especially if you're working in the kind of inner-city school where 98 percent of the student body is on subsidized lunches. You're supposed to feel sympathy and chalk up their problems to "the system" that has failed the students at every turn.

Easy enough for most teachers, perhaps; they didn't have Kayron.

He appeared innocuous at a glance, a short, pudgy Jamaican kid with long, feminine eyelashes. Other than a perplexing propensity for wearing cargo shorts year round, even when the weather called for his black NorthFace parka, nothing seemed amiss; he was even one of the rare ninth-graders who cared enough about getting a good grade to complete his work (doing the bare minimum, mind you, but still doing it) and to turn it in close to on time. That alone was usually the mark of a "good" kid.

But his teachers knew better.

"Poor you—you have a 'Kayron class,'" teachers would say to me sympathetically, looking at my attendance roster across the table in the faculty lounge.

"Kayron, you know you have a lot of potential," I told him one day.

"Oh, I know, Miss," he assured me without taking his eyes off the Gameboy that I had asked him to put away at least ten times.

"And, you know, you do a lot more homework than many of your classmates do . . ."

"Yeah, they don't really have much going on up here." He pointed to his head.

"So, you'll be happy to know that I'm giving you an 80 in my class," I told him.

"I know, Miss."

"How do you know?"

He sighed, turning to his friend Leslie and rolling his eyes. "Sometimes I really wonder about her . . ." he said. Then, as if I hadn't heard his aside, he told me, "Miss, it's obvious. Would you look at the amazing work that I do in this class?"

———

Kayron's work was not nearly as amazing as he thought it was.

We were studying Romeo and Juliet. I had asked the students to make a poster advertising the play. "Juliet is the rose, that without sunlight, or Romeo's love, will wilt like a flower and die, and the rain is the nourishing party that makes their love come alive," wrote Kayron on poster-sized paper. He proceeded to draw some pictures of roses and sunlight in bright Crayola tones, with rays that said things like "hope" and "joy" streaming out of the poster at every edge.

"That's very . . . creative," I told him, wondering if he had, in fact, read the play.

"I know. It's the best. So we're just going to put it up right here in the middle, where everyone can see it," said Kayron. He took my roll of tape out of my hands and proceeded to post his paper in the middle of our class board, covering up several student essays from the other classes.

Later that day, the tape became un-sticky, and one side of his picture fell, leaving it hanging lopsided on the board. Kayron raised his hand while I was in the middle of a lesson on grammar.

"Miss Garon?" he said, and then repeated "Miss Garon! Miss Garon!" when he saw that I was doing my best to ignore him. I gave in.

"Yes, Kayron?"

"My poster. It's lopsided." At this, the other kids yelled "Kayron, shut up!"

"Okay, we'll fix it later."

"Miss Garon, you know this is the best work anyone in this class did." At this, the rest of the class groaned. "You should be jumping up to fix it right now. What kind of a teacher are you?"

———

I was giving a quiz on grammar. Not having paid attention during the lesson, Kayron was unprepared, and he knew this. I had just seated the students in rows when Kayron started inching his desk over toward his pal, Leslie.

"Kayron, move away from Leslie."

"Why, Miss Garon?" he whined.

"Because your desk is too close to hers."

"You see how she's always picking on me?" he complained to Leslie, who giggled. Then he said, "Miss, I'm just sitting near Leslie so that I can get a piece of paper from her."

"Great, get your piece of paper and move your desk to the left."

I gave out the quiz. A minute later:

"Kayron! Get up and move across the room."

"But Miss Garon, why can't you be cool?"

"Because you're cheating off of Leslie's paper."

"What are you talking about? Leslie's not that smart—why am I going to cheat off of her paper? Hello?" He rolled his eyes. Leslie didn't object.

I went over to Kayron and dragged his desk across the room with him still sitting in it, much to his protests: "You're so un-cool, Miss! And look at your clothes! They're hideous!" He remained where I had put him, though for the next few minutes I heard him muttering "just mad about how she can't afford designer jeans" and "damn teacher needs a push-up bra."

I looked down at my clothes. I was wearing sneakers, khakis, and a light green polo shirt. *Do I need a push-up bra?* I wondered.

"Miss, I need to get out a notebook to put my paper on," he piped up. He still hadn't started the quiz.

The other students groaned: "Miss Garon, can you make him shut up? He's mad annoying."

"Kayron, you don't need your notebook. Can you please take this quiz quietly?" I asked him.

"Okay Miss, you won't hear any more out of me, I promise."

A minute later, I caught him peeking into his notebook, which he had removed from his backpack surreptitiously. I took his quiz away and gave him a zero. However, some weeks later, when I would calculate report card grades, I would find myself unable to get below a 65 for that kid—and as a result, I could never justify giving him the "F" I felt he deserved.

I still don't get how he always managed to pull that off.

————

"Miss Garon, I think you've noticed that my behavior has improved lately," Kayron told me after class one day, coming up to my desk and touching my shoulder fraternally, as he so often did when he was trying to butter me up. I instantly became wary.

"You think so?"

"Haven't you noticed?"

"Kayron, just yesterday you told Natesha that she should close her legs because the room smelled like fish. I don't consider that an improvement."

"But Miss Garon, that wasn't *at* you. It was at people in general. Why do you always have to be up in other people's business?"

"That doesn't matter. You just can't talk like that in class, Kayron," I said with as much patience as I could muster.

"But you noticed that I didn't use any inappropriate words, right?"

"The concept was still inappropriate."

"What do you mean? There wasn't a bad word in that sentence. It wasn't like last week, when I said all those words like 'c—t' and 'whore.'"

He had me there.

"Okay, if you behave well this whole week, I'll write you a note to bring home."

"No, you'll send it to the house in the mail."

"Oh really?"

"Miss." He rolled his eyes at me. "You know the letters that come in the mail are a lot more persuasive."

Two days passed. He was sedate the first day, but on the second he drew a picture on the desk of two people engaged in oral sex, and then pretended to find it and be shocked by it ("Oh my god! Look at this inappropriate drawing on my desk!"), thereby calling it to the attention of the rest of the·class. Fed up, I opened my classroom door and summoned the deans, who for once came promptly to remove him.

"You lying little fool," he hissed at me, as two deans shepherded him out of the room, gripping his elbows in case it occurred to him to make a run for it. The other students giggled.

Kayron came in several days later wearing an electronic device strapped to his wrist. "It's a calculator-watch, Miss," he told me. Then he sat down and proceeded to speak directly into it in a loud voice: "Danesha, can you hear me? What class are you in now?"

"Kayron, put the walkie-talkie away, we're starting now."

"But Miss, it's just a calculator." At this, the device crackled.

"Then why are you talking into it?"

"Miss, why do you have to be so un-cool?" Then he said to the "calculator," "Danesha, my teacher is making me turn it off now. Meet me after class!"

The next day Kayron arrived in class conversing into the walkie-talkie, and again tried to convince me that it was just a calculator. I marveled at how short he perceived my memory to be.

"Kayron, we had this conversation yesterday."

"I told you—I need it to do my math homework."

"You're not supposed to be doing math homework during English class anyway. Put it away."

He put it in his bag, grudgingly. Ten minutes later he went through his bag and found that the walkie-talkie was missing.

I sighed. "All right, guys, who stole Kayron's walkie-talkie? Can whoever took it please return it to him?"

"See Miss? This is your fault! Now you have to pay for it!"

"Kayron, you shouldn't have brought it to class in the first place."

"Yeah, well I'm just going to go right now and get you in trouble with my guidance counselor."

This particular group of guidance counselors, fortunately for me, had proven to be an ineffectual bunch. This I knew from trying to enlist their help dealing with students on numerous occasions. Whenever I reached out to them, they were on a coffee break, so I figured Kayron wasn't going to get any help from them, either.

After a few moments, the walkie-talkie resurfaced. It turned out that Anthony—with whom Kayron did not get along since he had passed around a drawing of Anthony performing oral sex on another classmate—had stuffed the walkie-talkie into his own bag. The walkie-talkie was returned, I threatened to call everyone's house (a threat I had little intention of honoring, since I'd never once gotten a response from either Kayron's or Anthony's parents), and at the end of class, Kayron approached my desk. I was about to say something about not bringing the walkie-talkie anymore, but he cut me off, pointed to his watch, and said in a patronizing voice, "You can't afford this, Miss, so don't even think about it."

———

A couple of weeks later, two other ninth-grade teachers persuaded me to help them plan a field trip to the *Intrepid*, a World War II aircraft carrier-cum-museum, with a lunch stop at McDonald's. Due to severe budget shortages at the school, we were informed by the administration that each of us could only pick ten students to bring on the trip. The rest would stay at school that day with a substitute.

"Whatever you do, don't pick Kayron," more than one teacher each told me. "There's no way in hell I'm going on a trip with that kid."

I made an effort to be secretive with the kids who were chosen, pulling them aside after class ("You're just talking to them because they're failing, right?" asked Kayron suspiciously when he saw them grouped around my desk), and telling them not to discuss the trip with their friends. Naturally, the entire ninth grade knew almost instantly.

Kayron was furious. "Miss! You know I'm the best student! Why didn't you pick me?" he yelled out in the middle of class.

"Kayron, I'll talk to you about this later," I told him, feeling the stares of the rest of the class upon us.

"No, now!"

The kids were doing group work. I pulled Kayron out into the hallway with me.

"First of all, there was a limit on the number of students we could bring—"

He interrupted. "It should have been me! You know I'm so much smarter than any of these people, like Megan and Leslie."

"You can't talk about your friends that way," I said, with as much patience as I could muster. "And besides, the choice wasn't just based on grades—it was based on overall behavior."

"What are you talking about? My behavior's great now."

Just two days prior, a teacher had stopped by my class to tell me that she had seen Kayron stealing school supplies from my desk drawer. Sure enough, when I had gone through my stuff, my stapler had been missing.

"C'mon, Kayron. I know you took my stapler."

"No! You lost it! Don't even try to blame that shit one me."

"Good grief, Ms. Medori saw you doing it! Okay, you know what? Never mind. The point is, you're not going, and that's that."

"What if your stapler turns up again?" he asked craftily.

"It better, or else I'm telling security you stole it. Now get back in the classroom," I told him, ushering him through the door.

Ten minutes later, Kayron "found" my stapler on the top of the supply closet, a spot I could never have reached on my own without the aid of a chair. "See, what would you do without me? Now you have to let me go on the trip!"

I ignored him.

But he kept pestering me about the damned trip.

"What if my mom comes with me?" he asked two days beforehand, in what he clearly believed to be a burst of inspiration. "Then can I come with you on the trip?"

"Sure, if your mom comes—then she can be responsible for you!"

Initially he seemed satisfied with this. But the next day, he came to me again. "So, what if my mom can only come meet me at the *Intrepid*? Can I just come down with you guys and then my mom will meet us there?"

I had seen this one coming a mile away.

"Kayron, I know what you're trying to pull! You cannot go on this trip unless a parent is with you throughout the duration. There's no way you're going to trick me with this."

"But Miss! Why are you so un-cool?"

I tried a different tactic.

"Kayron, why do you even want to go? You don't give a damn about the *Intrepid*. You'll have a substitute in English, so you can get away with not showing up. And you see these people every other day in school. Seriously, why does it matter to you?"

"Because you guys are going to McDonald's."

I burst out laughing. "So what? You can go to McDonald's any day you want, on your own!"

"But it's not the same!"

"Why not?"

"Because you're not there!"

This caught me off guard. I was about to say, "But you can't stand me!" and then I thought better of it. "Why do you want to eat lunch with me?" I finally asked.

At this, he became utterly exasperated. "God Miss, you have nothing going on up here at all!" he fumed, pointing to his head. Then he stormed out, leaving me in his wake.

―――――

Since he couldn't be there, Kayron appointed spies among the kids who were going on the trip. He outfitted each of his PI's with a disposable camera.

At first I didn't notice. I was distracted by one of the other students, an eighteen-year-old freshman named Damien who had confiscated a large bullet, a World War II relic that the tour guide was passing around to the group, and had snuck it into his backpack. We stopped the tour, and told all the kids to empty their stuff. The thief laughed, pulled the bullet out of his bag, and handed it over.

"Damien!" I hissed, pulling him aside from the tour. "I picked you for this trip because I thought you would behave! I can't believe you! This is a museum! How can you steal their artifacts?"

"Miss, chill, it was mad small," he replied, laughing, as if that cleared everything up. I couldn't figure out if he is talking about the bullet or about the crime itself. Then he ran off to jump on his friends from behind.

I became aware of clicking noises very close to me. I turned around. Leslie and Megan were angling Kayron's disposable cameras for close-up views of my behind. I made some faces at them, which they photographed gleefully. Then I told them to cut it out and join the rest of the group.

Twenty-four hours later, we were back in school, and Kayron had already developed the photos. I came into the classroom to find all the students gathered around his desk, laughing and pointing.

Kayron got up and came over to me, photo in hand. He put one arm around my shoulder and showed me the photo.

"See, Miss? That's you!" he told me, pointing at the picture. "God, I thought since you were leaving school, you'd at least try to look nice or something."

———

The remainder of my year with Kayron progressed in much the same manner. His top priority in life continued to be tormenting me. But as the term drew to a close, he begged me to give him my phone number and to tell him where I lived. I refused to do either.

"You have a stalker, Miss," the other kids laughed. I rolled my eyes.

The students' final day of school came around, and I thought that at last I would be rid of him. A week later, I exited the school on a sunny day. The campus was pretty quiet by that point. Teachers were the only people wandering the school halls; we were in the middle of grading state exams, so the students weren't in attendance. I was ravenous. I bought a sandwich at the local bodega and unwrapped it as I walked towards the Pelham Parkway station. I was bringing the sandwich toward my mouth when my innate clumsiness took hold—turkey, lettuce, and tomato fell out of the bun and landed on the sidewalk.

Instantly, I heard hysterical laughter. "You dropped your sandwich!" someone called to me. I looked up about thirty feet and saw Kayron standing on the top of the stairs to the elevated platform of the station's northbound side. He peered down at me through the bars in the railing. I noticed he was sporting his usual cargo shorts and white t-shirt, and thought how small he looked from this vantage point.

Sticking his arms through the bars, he waved at me.

"Kayron," I called up to him. "Can't you find someone else to follow around?"

"I liked you! You were the best teacher ever!"

"Come on," I called. "You're in tenth grade now. You don't need me anymore."

"But you need me!" he said, rolling his eyes. "Sometimes I really wonder about you. . . ."

Date: March 2, 2004
To: Family
Subject: In which hetero-normative gender roles become totally irrelevant . . .
From: Signature:

This is a good one:

I try to enter my classroom for twelfth period, but I'm blocked by this girl named Crystal, who keeps trying to rub up against me with her rear end. Weird. Once she lets me in, I barely have enough time to put my stuff down before she and Kayron start slugging the daylights out of each other for no apparent reason.

I step over them—they are rolling on the floor by this point—and go to the classroom phone to call security up to deal with this. My helpful students are chanting in the background "Kayron's fighting a girl! Kayron's fighting a girl!" I get hung up on. I dial again. Crystal hears someone say the word "Security" and, figuring correctly that she's about to get in trouble, leaps off Kayron and jets from the room. Kayron sits back down in his seat as if nothing has happened. Two minutes later, security—in the form of a lone school safety officer—arrives at the door to my classroom.

"What's the deal?" the school safety officer asks, looking bored.

"Kayron and Crystal had a fight," I say.

"You started a fight with a girl?" the officer asks Kayron incredulously.

Kayron shrugs. The security guard asks where Crystal is, and I tell him she ran away. "She's wearing a pink coat," Crystal's best friend tells the officer. I love the loyalty here. The officer tells Kayron to get his stuff and hauls him to room 125, the security office, where he tells me to send Crystal in the unlikely event that she should return.

I try to restart the lesson. I get maybe thirty seconds into it when there's a knock at the door. It's Crystal. "You're supposed to be in room 125," I tell her. "Oh," she says, and walks out of the classroom again. I look into the hallway for a dean or school safety officer to make sure she actually goes there, but seeing as there are none, I decide just to try and continue with the lesson.

Just then, a different school safety officer shows up at the door. "Do you know where Crystal is?" he asks me.

"She ran off before your other guy got here—didn't they tell you?"

"She's wearing a pink coat," the students say with glee. "And she beat up Kayron."

"Kayron got beaten up by a girl?" the officer asks in disbelief. Then his eyes light up, and he says, "Oh, is he the really gay one?"

"No, that's Cookie," says one kid. "But Kayron's gay, too," adds another. The security guard looks at me with raised eyebrows. "Is this, like, the gay class?" he asks. "Uh . . . I'm not sure," I say.

Suddenly, Natasha screams. "Natasha!" I say. Her scream is loud enough to draw the attention of the assistant principal, who happens to be wandering down the hallway at that moment. He comes in. "What's the problem?" we ask, as she jumps out of her seat, runs across the room, and starts hitting a seventeen-year-old punk named Brandon, who barely ever attends class and, when he does, insists that he is "VIP."

"Brandon's tearing Kayron's journal," Natasha yells. I look over and realize that she is correct, though why that warrants screaming on her part, I have no idea. Kayron must have left his journal behind when he was brought down to room 125 and now ripped pages of it are strewn all over the floor. "Brandon! What's your problem???" I say, but that's the only thing I can think of because, to be honest, I'm stunned.

The assistant principal says to Brandon, "Get your stuff. You're out of here." Brandon mimics him, saying in a prissy voice, "Get your stuff, you're out of here," and the students giggle. I say in horror, "Brandon! This is the assistant principal! You can't mess around with him like that!"

"Then what the f—k is he doing in this class?" Brandon says. "Get that motherf—r out of here!"

"Brandon!" I say, shocked. The assistant principal is livid. "Get your stuff!" he yells again.

"But I'm VIP," says Brandon.

The assistant principal looks confused.

"Brandon, just go with him, please," I say.

"But Miss, I'm VIP," he repeats genially. The kids are laughing now.

At this point, I've had enough, and I say something I really shouldn't. "You're VIP of *what* exactly???" I ask him. "Of people who are seventeen and still acting like fools in ninth-grade English?"

He seems completely unfettered by this remark, and as he exits the classroom surrounded by security guards he says, "I know! What's the problem with this place?"

I keep wondering the same thing.

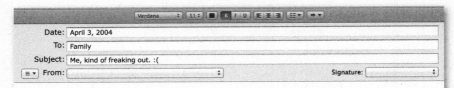

Two months ago, I gave a quiz to my ninth-grade English class wherein I used the word "punks" and the term "jack sh_t" (spelled that way, intentionally incorrectly) to slyly signal the wrong answer on a multiple-choice question. I agree that it was excessively bad judgment—I don't remember what I was thinking, save that I was trying to be exacting but with a sense of humor. Now I feel like a complete idiot. I guess the gravity of subtly cursing on paper didn't occur to me; bear in mind that these kids are fifteen/sixteen, and this is the class where I've had to discipline students for calling me a "cock-sucking whore." Also I'd seen other quizzes (from other teachers) where students had been referred to jokingly as "suckers," and where references had been made to marijuana, and I guess I figured if those kinds of things were acceptable then my quizzes were probably okay.

Yesterday, at 5:45 p.m., the principal and the assistant principal called me into their offices and gave me this lecture about how some parent complained to them about my quiz, how I'm "defacing the name of teaching" (they literally said this), and said I have to write a letter to *all* the parents and apologize to them for offending them.

Since the parents who came to parent-teacher conferences all told me what a good teacher I was and how glad they are that their kids have me, I am kind of upset at the thought of embarrassing myself and undermining my authority with *all* of the parents. I'd rather speak to the complaining parent one-on-one rather than inviting all the parents to criticize my quizzes.

I am ticked off at this whole school. As my Teaching Fellows mentor pointed out a few months ago, it's an organizational nightmare. I've had problems with sexual harassment from faculty members, which I took straight to the principal, who then said she'd make an announcement at the next faculty meeting, but never did.

I also think the mentoring system is a joke: Joe, my in-school mentor, had to drop me when baseball practice started because he's coaching.

I'm beginning to think that perhaps I should switch to a new school if I can and get a fresh start. Maybe I would be better off in a middle school; the line of appropriateness would be less confusing for me because the kids would be younger. I'm going to be wary of what I put on my quizzes from now on, I'm going to write whatever letters to parents they tell me to, and I'm going to just try and be a model teacher. But I feel like they're out to get me here, and I'm so scared.

Date: April 5, 2004
To: Family
Subject: Trying to save my own ass . . .
From: Signature:

My letter to the parents after the quiz incident (with my private notes to David, another teacher, in italics):

Dear Parents,

It came to my attention on the eve of Spring Vacation that some of you objected to the language that I used in a quiz I administered to your children several weeks ago [*a make-up in response to their all having failed the first quiz on the Harlem Renaissance . . . like I said—punks!*]. Looking back on this quiz, I am embarrassed at my lack of judgment, and I want to apologize for any discomfort or insult that I may have caused you and your children. Please know that I meant no offense and will do whatever it takes to rectify this mistake on my part.

Your children will tell you that, though I am a demanding teacher, I am also a fair teacher who cares about them immeasurably and seeks to use humor as a means of encouraging them to take their studies more seriously. However, I deeply regret the poor example I set for the students. [*Note the fact that I avoided taking digs at them for not attending parent-teacher conferences and for one of their kids calling me a "c—k-sucking whore" in the middle of class. Go self-restraint.*] I encourage you to please contact me in the English office if there is anything you would like to discuss with me concerning my teaching or your child's performance in English 2. You can also send a note with your child that tells me when would be a good time to call you. We are partners in your children's education; please let me know what I can do to hold up my end of the bargain.

Sincerely Yours,

Ilana Garon

CHAPTER FOUR

Kenya & Crystal

Part I: The Research Question

I decided late one night, when I was drinking a beer and staring at the ceiling, that if my students were to graduate from ninth grade without ever having written a research paper, I'd be a failure as a teacher. So the next day I gave them their first ever research assignment. The sheet I'd created that morning instructed them to find a subject in which they were interested, write about how they became interested in this subject, research the subject in a library, and then interview an expert on the subject.

"Your topic shouldn't just be a subject—like, baseball—it should include a research question," I told them. "And that should be a question that isn't a yes-or-no kind of thing, but something deeper. Like, my research question could be 'What is the history of baseball?' or 'What is the role of women in baseball?' or something like that. You want it to be sort of focused. Now, can someone give me another example of a good research question?"

Immediately, the hands flew into the air.

"Yes, Kenya."

"Why do only white people get abducted by aliens?"

I burst out laughing. "That's a great question, but I don't know how you're going to research that. Let's try something a little more . . . down to earth."

"Why do only white people get anorexic?" she offered.

"Okay, maybe something away from the white people . . . yes, Carlos."

"Football!"

"Alright, that's a good start. But remember what we said about how it had to be a question . . ."

Carlos thought for a minute. "Like, 'What is football?'"

"Closer. You're getting there. Think about some part of it that is specific—something that you could really research . . ."

One of the kids yelled, "SEX!"

I'd been waiting for that one.

"Yeah, that's fine," I told him, much to the class's shock and awe. "But you better have a good research question, or else . . . I'll call your mom and read your paper to her . . . *capisce*?"

"Noooo! Miss! That's OD!"

I gave a quiz later that week, in which the kids had to identify the good and bad research questions in the bunch. Here were the choices:

1) Why does the locker room smell bad after gym?
2) What was the role of African Americans in World War II?
3) Is Ms. Garon's class the most awesome one in the school?
4) What is hockey?
5) Are drugs good or bad?
6) What do teenagers know about the transmission of HIV?

———

Part II: The Experts

I had told the students they had to speak to someone who was an expert on their chosen topic.

"So how am I supposed to call up Michael Jordan to ask him about basketball?" one of the kids asked, irritated.

"Okay, great question," I said. "I think we have to revise the meaning of the word 'expert' for the purposes of this project. Say you're doing a report on something relating to sports . . . who's someone you might be able to interview about that?"

A hand went up. "Yes, Miguel."

"A gym teacher?"

"That's perfect. Great idea. Okay, say you're doing a report that has to do with health, or diseases. Who might be a good person to talk to about that?"

Dead silence in the room. Then, one quiet girl, Nicola, raised her hand. "Maybe I could ask my sister? She's a nurse," she said, barely above a whisper.

"Nicola, that's perfect. Thanks for helping us out with that."

We went around the classroom and discussed whom each student might interview for his or her respective project. Someone's uncle was a police officer—perfect for a paper on crime in the area. Someone's mom worked in a real estate office—a reliable source, I hoped, for a paper about the criteria for living in a housing project.

Ranfi, one of the class's Resource Room kids, asked, "What about drugs, Miss? Can I ask Mr. Porteno?"

Mr. Porteno was a special education teacher.

"Why is he an expert?" I asked.

"Because he's done all of them, Miss. He told me. Can I interview him?"

Demetrius, a football player who, for all his brawn, defied all stereotypes by being smart and sensitive, raised his hand and asked, "What if you're doing that one about teenagers and what they know about STDs?"

Someone hooted across the room, "Yo, Demetrius, ask your mom!"

"Hey now—none of that!" I said. The kids kept laughing, so I sat down on my desk and crossed my arms. In a moment they quieted down.

"I think Demetrius is wondering about something we should all consider," I told them. "And I think a lot of you might want to research topics that will force you to ask difficult questions. Which means we've got to practice . . ."

Part III: The Interview

I set up two desks facing each other in the middle of the room. Then I had the rest of the class gather around us, fishbowl style. I looked around for someone who wasn't paying attention to be my first victim.

"Crystal, come help me demonstrate how we do an interview," I said.

"Ooooh, Miss. Are you picking me?"

The correct spelling of Crystal's name, as written on the official attendance record (though Crystal herself never wrote it that way), was "Crystle"—an obvious misspelling by what I suspected was a teenage mother. She was a strange, feisty girl who tended to start fights with boys.[1] Periodically she would start laughing uncontrollably in the middle of class, and no one would have any idea why.

"Yeah, you. Come sit at the desk that's facing me."

I pointed at the seat opposite me, and Crystal sat down.

"Okay, guys," I said, addressing the class, who were all watching in fascination now. "I'm pretending that Crystal is my expert, and I'm interviewing her."

I turned to Crystal. "Good morning, Ms. Crystal," I said to her, in an emphatically slow, polite, stage voice.

"Oooh, Miss. You're turning me on."

"Crystal! If you can't participate maturely, I'm sending you out. Are you ready to behave?"

"Yeah, Miss, go on."

---

1   As witnessed in the journal entry for March 2, 2004.

"Okay, good." I cleared my throat and began again. "Good morning, Ms. Crystal." I shook her hand, all the while looking meaningfully at the students to make sure they were noticing my gesture. They were riveted. "How are you doing today?"

"Gooooood . . ." Crystal said, in a sensual voice. I ignored it.

"Great. My name is Ms. Garon, and I'm doing a research paper on . . ." I hadn't thought that far ahead yet. "On the Middle Ages."

"Yo, Miss! That's mad boring!" the students groaned in unison.

"Okay, fine! I'm researching STDs. Better?"

"Yeah!" they all yelled.

"Great. Now, Ms. Crystal," I said, returning to my stage-voice. "I'm doing a research paper on STDs, and I wondered if, as a nurse, you might be able to answer some of my questions."

"Ohhh, yessss!" Crystal said. She sounded as though she was intoxicated, and her eyes were shining a little too brightly.

"So, yeah . . . my first question is: What is the rate of HIV transmission in high schools—" I froze. Crystal was learning toward me over the desks. It took me a few seconds before I realized that she was puckering her lips and heading towards mine. I turned at the last second. Her kiss landed wetly on my cheek.

"Crystal! You can't make out with me! I'm your teacher!"

The class, silent only a moment before, was now in hysterics.

"But I love you, Miss!" she announced brightly, much to the amusement of her friends.

"And I'm very glad you're in my class, Crystal," I said to her. "But you can't kiss teachers. It's not appropriate."

"But I like girls!"

"Okay, and I fully support that decision. But I'm still your teacher, and you just can't do that to me. Okay?"

"Okay," she sighed.

Just then the bell rang. Crystal's dejection abated instantly, and she ran, cackling, out into the hall to join her friends.

————

Part IV: The Writing

The thing was, after all that effort, very few of the kids ever turned in their papers. I spent hours in class working with them one-on-one, helping them come up with introductions, with interview questions, with surveys to give to their classmates, with library research . . . and still, when the day came, the results were pitiful.

"Natasha," I said, when one girl turned in an essay that had obviously been plagiarized, "I know you didn't write this."

"Oh yeah? Prove it," she said.

"Sure thing. Tell me why your essay still has hyperlinks in it, and a link to Wikipedia at the bottom of the page."

Several students, who had been watching, yelled "Ohhhh, snap!" and started laughing.

I called Natasha's mother. "Your daughter can't turn in assignments like this," I said. "It's unacceptable to plagiarize."

"Well, what did you want her to do? You said it was due today," her mother said.

Another kid, Tyrell, who was on some other planet and would later be expelled for setting another kid's hair on fire "to find out what would happen," gave me a disk. "My printer's not working," he said.

I opened his disk on the library computer later that day, and all I could find on it were photos of basketball players.

"Tyrell, what is this?" I asked him.

"That's my research."

"So where's the rest of your paper?"

"That's it."

I implored them to turn in their papers. "Turn them in late," I said. "It's still better than nothing. Please guys . . . for me." But few kids turned in anything at all, and most of the stuff they did turn in was taken directly off the Internet. I ended up counting the paper for one-eighth of their grade, instead of one-fourth, as I'd planned. Frustrated nearly to the point of tears, I took out my disappointment on the kids, telling them that if they didn't get their act together, they'd never graduate. Then, after they left, I sat at my desk with my head in my hands.

There was a small knock on the door. I looked up and saw Crystal grinning crazily at the window.

"Hey, you," I said, opening the door. And then, thinking better of closing it with just the two of us in the classroom, I said, "No funny business now, okay?

"I just want to turn in my paper!"

I looked it over while she stood there. Considering most of the other ones I'd received, this one was actually decent. It was hand-written in pencil, with smears everywhere—but it was all her work. She'd written about the foster-care system and interviewed her foster mother.

"Crystal," I said. "This is really good."

I turned to her and saw that brightness in her eyes again.

"Crystal, don't even think about it! Go to your next class," I said, shooing her out.

———

Part V: Sources Cited

Shortly thereafter, Crystal had an incident involving sexual abuse at the hands of her foster father. She would be transferred to a new foster family, she told me one day at lunch. I was disappointed to see her go and confused about how—upon reporting sexual abuse—she hadn't been removed more promptly. She left the school at the end of the year.

Mr. Porteno turned out not to be an expert on drugs—at least, not by his own account. Actually, he had been a foot soldier in the Vietnam War, which seemed more interesting. I never did find out how Ranfi came up with that other idea.

And Kenya did a research paper on Roswell, New Mexico, which—although largely cribbed from dubious Internet sources—

was admittedly rather entertaining. Although, in the course of her paper, she never did explain why it is that aliens only ever abduct white people.

That part remained for me to find out.

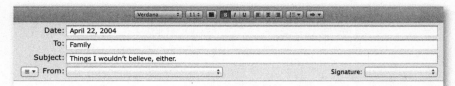

Here are some interesting things that have happened this week:

1) Sex bracelets. This is a disgusting new fad with the kids. Basically, they
   wear these multi-colored rubber bracelets—there are about twelve
   to fifteen different ones—and each color represents a certain sexual
   act. If someone comes and snaps your bracelet, you are supposed
   to perform the sexual act in question with that person. I find this
   incredibly disturbing, especially since one of the students gave me a
   color-key so now I know the specifics of what each bracelet means,
   and there are some things you just don't want to know about your
   students' lives. I gave each class a lecture about how just because
   someone snaps your bracelet, you are in no way obligated to do
   anything you wouldn't want to with them. I stressed this. The boys
   said, "Miss! Don't tell the girls that!" The girls said, "But why would you
   wear the bracelet if you didn't want to?" I feel like very few of them
   really have any feelings of self-worth or ownership over their bodies,
   and this is the root problem . . . this new fad is just symptomatic.

2) This one kid comes in with a bloody nose. "Miss, I need to go to the
   men's room," he says. "Yikes," I say and write him a pass to go out.
   Twenty minutes later I notice a vial of red food coloring on the desk
   of one of his peers. When I make the connection, they all crack up
   laughing. The kid with the "bloody nose," meanwhile, doesn't return
   all period. I kind of have to give him credit: I would never have gone to
   that much effort to cut class when I was in high school.

3) Several of my ninth-grade students have taken to calling me "Mommy."
   They come in and say "Hi Mommy" and throw their arms around my
   waist. It's a little odd. I pointed out to one girl that since I'm not even
   twenty-three, I would have had to be seven or eight years old when
   I gave birth to her. "But you're kind of like a Mommy," she said. When
   I asked how, she said it's because I give the kids candy, quarters to
   use the phone when I can spare them, and I let them hang out with
   me while I prepare for my classes. The fact that these things qualify

you to be a parent, in their eyes, is a little off-putting . . . especially since today, when I met some of them on the subway, they asked me completely earnestly if the reason I don't own a car is that I'm not old enough to have a driver's license.

4) One of my favorite students, who had an abortion last term, is pregnant again. This will be her second abortion in three months, and her third in her life. (She had her first at thirteen.) I am torn between feeling really annoyed at this girl (who is smart enough to know better!), and just depressed by the whole situation.

I'm tired. Must sleep now.

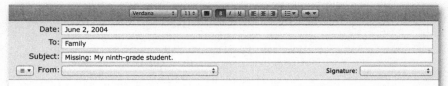

One of my students has gone missing. This happened last semester, as well, and the sixteen-year-old girl in question turned out just to have run off to a friend's house. Thus, I suppose I'm more blasé about it than I might be if this were the first time one of my students had ever gone MIA. Anyway, this kid (a fifteen-year-old girl named Emily) has been missing for three days. There are posters up all over our area of the Bronx with her picture, which is a little disconcerting to see—every time I pass one I think "Hey, that's Emily," and then I remember.

Cops—not just NYPD school safety officers—were in today to talk to my students, to see if they knew anything. The students aren't good at discerning what kind of information will be helpful, so the discussion with the cops largely turned into a gossip session about Emily's sexual proclivities, which I shortly put an end to. I also had to give the cops her folder, because it had some journal entries that someone hoped might be informative. So, what little privacy the kid had left has now been violated.

Rumors are that she may be hiding out with her twenty-two-year-old boyfriend, who lives up in Washington Heights, in an area that is reputed to be the "*Mecca* of crack dealership"; others say that she had a fight with her mom (who is allegedly too strict) and ran upstate. Nothing is very certain.

The police seem more concerned about this disappearance than they did about the previous one. I believe a lot of this has to do with the fact that this other girl's parents were fairly certain she had just run off, whereas Emily's mother doesn't have any idea. However, there is an added dimension: a twenty-one-year-old Julliard student disappeared in Inwood—one neighborhood north of where Emily may be hiding—on May 19th, and her body was found five days later. So now everything seems all the more serious as a result.

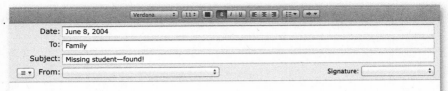

Date: June 8, 2004

To: Family

Subject: Missing student—found!

From: Signature:

Follow-up: The missing fifteen-year-old, Emily, was found safe and sound, apparently due to some tip that came from a member of my class. The anonymous kid went to security after the police officers came in and spoke to us and told them that he knew something, but hadn't wanted to say it aloud. Good to know people were paying attention. (Yes, Emily had in fact run away with the boyfriend to Washington Heights. She should be back in class any day now.)

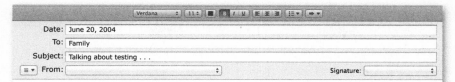

Date: June 20, 2004
To: Family
Subject: Talking about testing . . .
From: Signature:

The school year technically ended a few days ago. However, I have not had a moment to breathe yet, as Regents exams—state tests in all different subjects that the students have to take at prescribed times, in order to graduate high school—have been in full swing. Boy, do I hate proctoring. I sit around trying to think of exciting and creative ways to slip out unnoticed, because it is just so tedious! You're not allowed to read a book or anything while you're administering these tests, because you're supposed to watch the kids the entire time so that they won't cheat. And these tests are three hours long.

Then you have to grade them. That takes several days because in our school there are over one thousand students taking the English test, each test has four different essays, and each essay has to be read and graded by two people, three if there is a disagreement, and that doesn't even begin to address the multiple choice.

I got into an argument with two senior teachers who felt that I was grading their students too harshly.

"These are honor students; you can't give them a 2 [out of 6!]," they said.

"I'd be happy to look over any tests you feel I graded unfairly," I told them. "But that I am pretty sure I've been careful."

They proceeded to berate me about one particular kid's essay, which they insisted was "Four pages! And written by an honor student!" and thus should be given a higher grade.

I maintained that despite the length I didn't think it was a very good essay, and that there were other students whose essays I felt had been much better. "This essay is incomprehensible," I said.

"You can't grade down because of penmanship!" they retorted.

"I don't give a crap about penmanship! I'm downgrading because it contains incoherent sentences that could barely be construed as English!" I told them.

"You know what the kid means!" was their response.

This continued until Bill, the head of the English department, came over, took the essay, and read it.

"Well, I wouldn't have given this more than a three," Bill said.

"*What???*" the other teachers said, and proceeded to yell at him.

Bill put up his hand. "Just look at this sentence," he said. He read from the essay, "'Pollution is a factor in cumulus clouds. This is bad for humans. They.' See? This makes no sense! Come on," he said, putting the essay down. The senior teachers argued with him for a couple of minutes, but saw that they weren't getting anywhere. I was sweating and feeling vindicated. Then they turned on me and started making nice. ("We weren't trying to upset you, we just know you've never taught Regents, and we want to make sure you know how to grade. . . .")

For some reason, though I can argue with the best of them, I can never stand that feeling of being diminished. I burst into tears. It embarrassed me. I ran to the bathroom and washed my face.

Oh shit. I have to go back to grading, because the teachers I had a fight with just came into the teacher's lounge where I am writing this missive. More later.

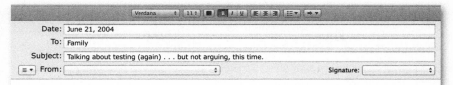

I wonder if we do the students favors by giving them passing grades, as we often do, for work that is so far below grade level. I really don't know what to make of it.

I had the students write research reports that they turned in the last day of term. One of the reports went like this: "I read a book about abortions. It had lots of information about abortions. If you ever get in trouble and need an abortion, you should read this book, because it will tell you what to do."

This went on for a paragraph (which was the entire first page of his paper, since he only had one paragraph per page), and I never managed to learn what the book was called, who the author was, or what allegedly good information the book disseminates.

And the crazy thing is, I passed this kid for the term (although I don't think he got more than a 55 on his report). He does the work, he comes to class, and he doesn't try to act like a badass. That counts for a fair amount here.

But then I wonder if I'm doing him a disservice by allowing him to slip by with this kind of work. But as I've probably said many times before, by the time the students get to me, they're so behind that this report on abortions was not the worst of the lot.

I was demoralized a while ago by a meeting with one of my mentors. She suggested that I haven't actually learned a darn thing about teaching, and am continuing to work in a failing school where all I do is discipline, because I'm terrified that if I'm actually expected to *teach*, someone will bust me on my ignorance. And the entire time she said this, I kept thinking, "Damn, she's on to me!" That is my secret fear. Everyone tells you all this corny stuff about how you're saving students' lives or whatever else, and you'd like to believe them, but the circumstances are so out of control that you eventually begin to feel that this whole business of "having an impact" is an illusion.

So why am I sticking it out? Well, for one thing, the vindication is *sweet*! On the last day of school, I busted my arch-nemesis student, Kayron, in a cheating scam. He was selling answers to his science final using a stolen exam. And the ridiculous thing is that he failed the test anyway! I know I shouldn't find this so humorous, but I haven't forgiven him for stealing my post-its, my tape, my scissors, all the blue markers, and two different staplers, all of which he was clever enough to pass off before I had any tangible proof of his involvement. Plus he was a pest the entire year and kept trying to put photos of me on the internet.

Anyway, it's summer break. There goes Year 1.

YEAR 2

Verdana   ⋮ 11 ⋮ ■ B i U ☰ ☰ ☰ ☷▾ ➡▾

Date: September 28, 2004
To: Family and friends
Subject: Maybe I should start a ninth-grade dating service . . .
≡▾ From: ⋮   Signature: ⋮

The best story so far:

This ninth-grader named Romaine (like the lettuce) is trying to ask out this other girl, named Christine, who sits next to him in class. She's having none of it. He begs, pleads, tells her she'll have the time of her life, that all he's asking for is *one date*. Christine says no. He appeals to me. (I might point out here that this kid is seventeen and has already done two years upstate for possession with intent to distribute—and here, he's trying to get me to facilitate his puppy love.)

"Miss, can't you convince her to go out with me?" he asks, right in front of her.

I shrug. "That's up to Christine, not me," I say. I look up and notice that he is wearing a necklace that says "Dominique" in ghetto-stylized lettering. "I have to say, though," I add, "If I were Christine, I'd probably wonder who Dominique is."

He looks defeated. "My daughter," he mumbles.

Yikes. "And how old is Dominique?" I ask, trying to recover smoothly.

"Two."

"So who takes care of her?"

He looks proud. "Me!"

"Um . . . okay, what about when you're at school?"

"Huh?"

"You know, you're obviously not leaving her in the locker. . . ."

"Oh, her mom."

"And how old is the mom?"

"I don't know . . . mid-twenties?"

There are so many things wrong with this picture. Christine comes up to me after class. "I don't really have to go out with him, do I?"

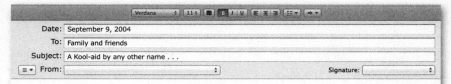

Date: September 9, 2004
To: Family and friends
Subject: A Kool-aid by any other name . . .
From: Signature:

My ninth-grade group is the class from hell; so far, they've threatened the life of their math teacher, and the deans keep coming in (sometimes accompanied by police officers) to pull out this kid who is quite large and wears a chill-pack on his back to keep him cool. The kids call this young man "Kool-aid," affectionately, and apparently he likes this name because he asked me to call him Kool-aid, as well, though I can't really bring myself to do so. (This other girl wants to be called "Beaver"—I'm not so keen on that one either.)

Seven classes currently take place there during a given period, which is even worse than the five last year. Periodically, the room erupts in cheers, and that's when we know a fight has started. Most recently, a student threw a paper ball at a teacher. When the teacher told him to get out, the student didn't budge, so in a moment of poor judgment, the teacher swatted at him. The kid thought the teacher was taking a punch at him, so he did what his "flight or fight" instincts dictated—he slugged back! The teacher's been absent since. I shouldn't find this amusing, but I do, because the teacher in question wrote me inappropriately sexual letters at the beginning of last year, and the student who hit him is one of my former repeaters.

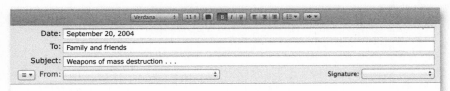

Date: September 20, 2004
To: Family and friends
Subject: Weapons of mass destruction . . .
From:
Signature:

We don't have enough chairs for all my students. Several of the chairs in one of my classrooms had bubble-gum all over them this Monday morning; the students refused to sit, so I called maintenance in to deal with it.

"Just have them put a piece of paper over the gum," the maintenance men said.

"I don't *think* so! You try telling my clothing-obsessed fifteen-year-olds that," I responded. The students, overhearing the conversation, said, "Yo, that's mad wack! Stop beastin' and give us some chairs, yo!" So we got our chairs, and that was good.

Last week, some grocery store near the school started selling these plastic eggs containing little toys—in this case, miniature guns that you assemble yourself and use to shoot rubber bands. So all my ninth-grade boys bought *loads* of these things (I bet they bought out the whole supply) and started shooting each other's faces during Advisory, which is basically group counseling in the form of a half-credit course. I asked them once to get rid of them, but every time I'd turn my back, they'd be shooting each other again. Finally, this kid named Sammy put his down on the table for a minute, and I ran and grabbed it before he could get it again. He asked for it back. I said no. He accused me of being "racis-sist." Go figure.

I brought this plastic gun to the dean of security. "I just thought you'd like to know what all the ninth-grade boys are coming to school with," I told him.

"Shit! That's a Level 5 security report!" he said. "They're not allowed to bring any kind of weapon, even a facsimile, to school. You're going to have to attend a court hearing."

"Shit!"

So all the deans barged into my classroom together during ninth period to "arrest" half my male students. They searched the boys' clothes and backpacks. The ones on whom they found the plastic guns (a few were smart enough to get rid of them) got some sort of note in their juvenile files, a hearing to follow, etc. Suspensions were given out. It was a wild time. The girls were thrilled. "That'll teach them to bring mad stupid toys to school," they said with obvious glee.

But the girls were not so innocent either. Friday morning, I had them all sitting at their tables doing work. Somehow, Felicia accused Quantisha of "copying." Quantisha gave her "a look." When you're a fifteen-year-old girl here, getting "a look" is the equivalent of being called a "pussy" for a fifteen-year-old boy. So words were exchanged. It was about to come to blows. "I'mma stab you in the *face*!" said Quantisha to Felicia. The girls stepped out into the hallway at the end of the period. They started removing their jewelry, giving their rings and name-necklaces to their "handmaidens" to hold for them during the fight that was seconds from ensuing.

"Um . . . I don't think so," I said. I grabbed the key players from one faction and brought them into the class. "You guys are going to wait ten minutes and cool off before you go to math," I told them. I made them sit down and relax while I gathered up papers, put things away, etc.

"Are they fighting in your class?" I asked their history teacher later.

"They are!" he told me. "Wanna send 'em to peer mediation?"

We went down and made the referral. The peer mediators, all twelfth-graders assisted by guidance counselors, went around and pulled everyone out of class. They listened to every side of the story. Eventually a "contract" was written up.

Two of the girls came to see me later that day. "So that contract was satisfactory?" I asked them.

"Yeah, it's great! If Quantisha looks at us one more time, we get to beat her up!" they said gleefully.

And so it goes . . .

CHAPTER FIVE

Felicia

Her name was Felicia, and I taught her in my second year of teaching, when I was twenty-three. Her parents were having a reverse custody battle over who didn't have to take care of her. The odds of her being totally screwed up by this were astronomical. But she smiled. She played. She said funny, witty things. She teased me for things I had never told the students (hell, was wary of even thinking about)—"Miss, you blush whenever Chris walks into the room. He's cute, right?"—and she would be right on the money, because I did have a totally mortifying crush on Chris the security guard with all his chains and crazy tattoos and dreams of being a rap superstar. Then she would link arms with me confidentially, knowing she was right, and smile.

At fourteen, she was no taller than four feet, ten inches, with curly light-brown ringlets and gray eyes, a tiny, explosive little firebrand with a sharp tongue and a quick smile. When I could get her to stand still, I'd try to ask her about her life—mainly how her classes were going, or what boys she was interested in. And she would turn it on me like lightning, and start guessing—alarmingly good guesses, often.

"So are you going to go out with José? He has a huge crush on you," I would say.

She would reply, "Oh, what a coincidence that you should ask, since you're the one getting your ass stared at by Mr. Marcus every time you walk down the hall! Yeah, don't even lie—I know who those flowers were from! Anyway, so let's talk. Are we your favorite class, or is eighth period? You can tell me. I already know we're the only class you brought donuts for last Friday!"

To some degree, I reluctantly confided in her. You never confide in students. It is one of the cardinal rules of teaching. But she solicited these confidences so easily. It was so natural and quick to tell her something: "Okay, you're right, Mr. Marcus did give me the carnations. But he's twice my age, and I'm not interested, and I'm terrified of getting the rumor mill started—so don't tell anyone about that, or about the donuts, okay?" She would nod her head understandingly and put her little hand on top of mine.

School required no academic effort of her. She was already in a class of exceptionally bright kids; they were far and away the most intelligent and motivated group of freshmen I have ever taught. Felicia was in another league. During the first month of school, she told me she was bored with the young adult novels in the library, so I gave her Alice Sebold's *The Lovely Bones*. She finished it in two days ("It's the best book I *ever* read, Miss!") and moved on to Jeffrey Eugenides's *Middlesex*, which she disliked, but finished and understood enough to come in and recount for me the various ways in which Eugenides needed a better editor.

"Seriously, this shit's about one hundred pages too long," she told me. I had liked *Middlesex* a lot, but there was no denying she had a point.

She should have been enrolled in some kind of Gifted and Talented center. She had, in fact, taken the test and qualified for specialized high school placement, but her parents (in a typical fit of irresponsibility) had given their then thirteen-year-old the burden of independently choosing and enrolling in a high school. So she had picked the one closest to her home—ours, with its rock-bottom test scores and constant police patrol—and gone there. She made solid grades—not what she was capable of, but solid. I tried to encourage her to make an extra effort, citing the incentive of college scholarships for motivated minority kids. And she would just look at me with this expression of "Get real, Miss." Defeat? Apathy? Disdain? A little bit of all three? I was never sure.

———

Early that fall, a flyer advertising a high school poetry contest was put up in our department office. I mentioned it to the class, and the next day Felicia brought in a poem to enter. Its title was something along the lines of "Why I'll Be a Divorce Statistic at Twenty-Five." She turned it in quite willingly, and that surprised me, because her writing perhaps demonstrated more vulnerability than anything else she would ever have exposed voluntarily.

In the hopes of enticing other students to enter, I made her read her poem aloud in class. She was a cool kid; maybe if the kids saw that she was entering, they would want to do it, too.

Usually they listened to whatever she said. The boys were all in love with her, and the girls were all afraid she would kill them, in light of Felicia's calm threat to a girl who had "trash-talked" her: "Listen, bitch, I swear to God I will stab you in the heart with a pen if you ever do me like that again, you feel me?" But that day they were tired, preoccupied. Maybe it was too close to Christmas break. Regardless, they didn't pay attention. She stood up in front of the chalkboard, reading her divorce poem to a class of thirty kids, all of whom were talking, throwing paper balls at each other, passing notes, and generally acting like the fourteen-year-old goofballs that they were.

She looked up and stopped midsentence. The other kids didn't notice. She stamped her little foot on the linoleum, registering her impatience, but they kept on talking, acting like she wasn't even there. I yelled at them, but my belated intervention, while it sobered them, didn't do much for her. She looked at me forlornly, and then gave up entirely.

"That was discouraging, Miss," she whispered to me as she slunk back to her seat. The other kids didn't notice.

After class she handed me a sad, crumpled little piece of paper and I took it home, where I typed it, spell-checked it, and sent it to the contest with a $10 check and a letter explaining that the kid who wrote this poem was from an inner-city school and to please give her the recognition I felt she deserved.

(In point of fact, we would never hear back from the contest. It was probably a scam; I can only conclude that they took the entry fee I paid on her behalf and fled the country.)

She asked me about it, though, a couple of times. "When do you think I'll hear from the contest, Miss?" she asked me. It was her study hall period, and I had come barging in because, peering through the window in the door of the classroom, I had seen her sitting uncharacteristically alone. The other kids were looking over at her, confused. Why didn't she want to play? I walked in and brought myself down to her, desk level. "When will the contest let us know, Miss?" she asked. It was December then; I said I hoped April, maybe May. I didn't know for sure. I asked her if she was okay. She smiled at me, but there were tears in her eyes. She refused to tell me why.

———

The semesters changed, and suddenly I was not her English teacher anymore. I was working with tenth-graders that term, and it was difficult, because they were a rowdy bunch, and by an unfortunate coincidence, all male. I had been assigned to them on the heels of a beloved teacher—a benevolent ex-baseball player aptly named Claus—who had been very "cool" with them, as they put it. Now that he was on a semester-long leave for shoulder surgery, I was teaching the class. It often felt like they were angry with me purely for not being him.

"What can I do to make you guys not hate me so much?" I asked one day, exasperated. For the past few days they had been throwing baby carrots, stolen from the lunchroom, at my back every time I turned to write on the board. I could never whirl around fast enough to catch the culprits.

"We don't hate you," they told me. "We just miss Claus."

One of the toughest guys, a kid named Alberto who was a foot taller than I was and about twice my weight, looked at me with a pained expression. "Mister Claus . . . Miss, no one was like him. He was just like this cool older brother," he said wistfully.

When he said this, I felt like crying.

In light of my ambivalent relationship with the boys, it seemed all the more important to maintain some vestige of closeness with the class that Felicia was in, a class that, I believed, loved me the way the boys loved Claus. I came to their advisory class one morning to say hello. Felicia greeted me with her characteristic charm—"Do you miss us, Miss Garon?"—but she seemed distracted.

It was around that time that I found out how much her grades were slipping. Her history teacher was the one who told me. "She's pulling a 'D' in my class," he said. "She isn't doing any homework and she basically failed the last test."

I had never seen Felicia break a sweat. She already knew so much. She watched and understood *The Daily Show* at fourteen. She made jokes about Communism and wore a Che Guevara shirt when most of her peers couldn't have identified Latin America on a map. She was so much more sophisticated, more worldly than they were. How on earth was she failing freshman history?

I went to her guidance counselor to see what was up. "Yeah, she's gone down in everything," the counselor said. She probably was not even supposed to tell me that, the counselor, but she did anyway.

I pulled Felicia from class during her lunch period. I was professional. "You wanna tell me what the hell is going on, girl?"

She rolled her eyes. "I'm not seven."

"Right. You're fourteen going on twenty-eight. Answer my question."

"Miss, don't you think you're just insecure about your role as a young teacher?"

"Woah, this isn't about me! We're talking about you."

"Why do you care, Miss?" Exasperation.

"Because I do. Because you're brilliant, and you know it, and I hate seeing you slip like this."

"Can I go now?"

"Yeah. Just try and pick your grades up a little, okay? And come see me if you want to talk. . . ."

She scampered off.

————————

I kept my distance. I tried to give her the space she clearly wanted, as much as it worried me to see her grades going down the toilet. If she had looked happy, maybe it would not have bothered me so much. But when I saw her in the halls, though she was always surrounded by friends, she would laugh with bitterness that I didn't recognize. She had stopped coming to see me altogether.

So I went into her advisory class again, ostensibly to see how *all* the kids in that class were doing. She was in the back of the room, goofing off. Her sleeves were rolled up, and on one of her wrists, there was a little tree. Just like that—a neat little tree carved into her skin, the angry welts having been reduced to perfect red branches.

I came over and picked up her wrist. "What is this?"

She immediately pulled away, moved her wrists out of sight. "Nothing."

"That's not nothing.'"

"My cat scratched me." Sleeves rolled up. Hands tucked under her arms.

"That's one hell of an artistic cat."

She laughed sardonically. "You know it is."

————————

As a teacher, I'm a mandated reporter: legally obligated to inform the guidance counselors if I see a student in a potentially harmful situation. I gave the word. They had her in the guidance office fifteen minutes later.

————————

As I expected, she was livid. First, she told the guidance counselors that I was a liar and an idiot. She wouldn't let them see her arms. Then she told them I was stalking her. That hurt. "It's pretty common for them to say stuff like that," the guidance counselor told me by way of comfort. "Kids who have never had anyone care about them in their lives don't know how to handle it when someone demonstrates that they do." Somehow, that just made me feel worse.

In the hallways, if I saw her, she would turn and run the other way. She wouldn't even make eye contact with me or look in my direction. I eventually started taking a different stairwell so that I wouldn't have to run into her anymore.

One of her friends came to find me. "She's really mad at you, Miss," Jennifer said. She said this with a note of glee. Jennifer liked drama. Jennifer also liked having someone who was as miserable as she was; she, too, was a veteran of self-mutilation, but I'd only learn that much later.

"I know," I said. I gave Jennifer a book to borrow. "You can let Felicia read it when you're done, if she wants to."

"She's really pissed. She, like, hates you."

I sighed. "Well, tell her I still care about her, and that if she wants to come and scream at me in person, she's welcome to."

I talked to another English teacher about it. "Leave your door open," he said. "You did the only thing you could do, by law. So just leave your door open. Eventually she'll come back."

The math teacher and the history teacher both tried to intervene. "Ms. Garon loves you. She cares about you. That's why she did what she did."

"I f—ing hate that bitch," Felicia said to them. "She better leave me alone."

The worst part was that the rest of my special, smart, talented class turned on me, too. Graffiti appeared on the walls: "Miss Garon is a snitch." I could have pled that this wasn't the same as ratting out a peer, that I'd done it because I cared about Felicia, or that it was illegal not to. But I didn't bother.

Except for once. Another student in that class, Naomi, confronted me online. I'd given the kids my screen name so that they could ask me questions when they didn't understand their homework assignments. So Naomi sent me an instant message saying, "You're a snitch."

"Naomi," I typed back, trying to rationalize with her, "This incident was not so clear-cut. I think Felicia needed help. I did it because I thought she was hurting, not because I wanted to get her in trouble or whatever."

"You helped no one," Naomi typed in response. "To hell with you."

She signed off before I could respond and copied and pasted the conversation on her MySpace page.

———————

Humiliated by my bad judgment (Who in their right mind tries to rationalize with angry fourteen-year-olds?) and a little bit afraid that I would incur someone's wrath (administrators or other students, I wasn't sure), I went and talked to the social worker who was counseling Felicia by this point.

"I know you can't tell me anything about her," I said to him, "but I just don't know what to do anymore. I wish they'd all stop hating me. I wanted to help her, and I feel like it's totally backfired."

Then I started crying. I had been holding it in for a while, but at that moment I realized how hurt and sad I was. I loved Felicia. That was the bottom line. And she hated me.

The social worker listened patiently.

"What is it you like about her?" he finally asked.

I thought about it. "I don't know. She's just so funny and cute. And so smart. I sort of see her as a little sister, I guess. I'm only a little bit older than she is, when you think about it, and we certainly have . . . well, had . . . a different kind of relationship than I have with most students."

He smiled.

"I've never counseled a student like Felicia either," he said. "She has this knack for creating drama. She's crafty: She'll ask me to tell teachers this, to tell the guidance counselors that, pit them all against each other to get everyone on her side. She's a nice kid, but she's a master manipulator. This is something it's important to know about her."

He paused and looked at me sympathetically.

"You have to be careful not to get too involved with kids like that," he said. "It's easy to do . . . all of her teachers have, basically. She's really good at luring adults into blurring boundaries."

I thought about that for a while. I was the adult here—how could I fault her for any of this? She was a really messed up kid; that was basically all I would cop to.

Besides, I still felt like a snitch.

"I'll stay away from her, ignore her, whatever she wants," I said. "But please tell me one thing: Will she eventually stop hating me?"

He smiled sympathetically. "You know I can't tell you that. We'll just have to see."

———————

I waited her out. I kept my door open, like the other English teacher had said, and I put the situation out of my mind. It was easier to do than I thought it would be. I became wrapped up with the class of all boys. I taught them Sex Education during Advisory that term, which was, weirdly, the event that finally bonded us all, despite their lingering sadness over Claus's departure. They were surprisingly eager to learn what I had to teach them and earnest about it. They really wanted to know about women. It was sort of sweet.

I took an old plastic box that had formerly held Twizzlers and cut an opening in the lid to the container. "Here's where you can put in any questions you have about sex that you're afraid to ask out loud," I told them.

The questions that came in the box were mostly along the lines of "Ms. Garon, will you marry me?" But it wasn't horrible. Spring came, the end of the year was in sight, and I started feeling happier again.

And apparently, around that time Felicia started to feel happier, too.

———————

It started small. Some of the kids were going on about how I was a snitch. Three full months later. They remembered everything, except their class notes on test day.

"Whatever. I'm over it," Felicia said to them. The history teacher told me about that later. And then another time, "It wasn't her fault. She had to tell. She was required by law."

(*That's my smart girl*, I thought privately when I heard.)

I still kept my distance. Felicia started asking me questions. Not to me directly—through other teachers.

"Felicia wants to know if you have more books she can borrow," her math teacher told me. "I said she should ask you herself, but then she just ran away."

A few weeks later, another thing happened. This, too, was told to me by the math teacher. Felicia came up to her after class and said, "I'm cool with Ms. Garon now."

"Well, that's great," said the long-suffering math teacher. "But does she know this?"

"I think so."

"Are you sure? Have you told her?"

"No."

"So how is she supposed to know?"

At that point, Felicia looked embarrassed again, and did what all adolescents do when they run out of things to say—rolled her eyes and stalked off.

————

The math teacher asked me to help her chaperone a field trip. "Felicia's going to be on it," she told me.

I was hesitant. "Is it cool if I come then?"

"Of course. I wouldn't have asked you if it weren't."

"But Felicia . . ." We still hadn't spoken in months.

"Yes, it's fine with her. I already asked."

I went to meet the kids after school, and Felicia ran up to me and threw her tiny arms around my waist, as if nothing had ever happened between us. "*Miss!*" she said, in her usual slightly bossy, conspiratorial tone. It was good to hear her voice again. "Your outfit is *so* last year. We have to do something about this. Now, let me tell you all about this drama I'm having with this boy named Jesus. . . ."

I guess that's fourteen-year-old speak for "I'm sorry." I certainly never pressed the issue. But just like that we were "cool." A few days later she called me on my cell (I had given it to her many months ago for her to call me if she was having problems) and left me a voicemail saying, "Miss Garon, this message is ridiculously dorky. 'At the beep, do your thing?' What the hell does that mean? You have to change it. Right now."

Summer came, then fall, and we were all back. I was teaching in a different school in the same building. But Felicia would occasionally come visit me to say hi, and tell me what was going on in her life. She told me that she had started to pick up her grades. We were not as close as we had been once, but I think that is the inevitable side effect of my teaching a different group of kids from year to year.

The last time I saw her was a couple of months at the end of her junior year. I was walking to the subway when I saw her goofing around with some friends a few blocks from the campus. She seemed, somehow, more grown-up than I had ever seen her: Her hair was straightened, and she had applied silver makeup flatteringly around her eyes. I was struck by how beautiful she had turned out to be. She ran up and hugged me, and said, "Are you dating that fat guidance counselor, Miss? Yeah, I saw you talking to him. What's going on with you two?" Then she cackled at my protestations.

I don't know that I have ever been as attached to a student as I was to her, and I don't know if I ever will be again. Perhaps it's healthier that way. But I still miss her.

Date: October 7, 2004

To: Family and friends

Subject: In which David takes down the Goliaths of our class . . .

From: Signature:

We're in ninth period, and the kids are taking their seats. Bryant, a chronic pain in the butt, decides he wants to sit where Pablo, a small kid, always sits. So he shoves all of Pablo's stuff off the desk to claim his territory.

Ian gets up and asks Bryant why he has no problem picking on small kids like Pablo, but won't fight anyone his own size. Bryant doesn't answer.

Ian touches Bryant on his chest and (lightly) sneers, "Pussy."

Bryant slugs him.

The fists start flying, and the classroom erupts into chaos. Everyone's screaming, running around, bumping into desks, trying to get out of the way of these *huge* guys who are slugging each other as hard as they possibly can. It doesn't help that the room is on a slant—seating is amphitheater-style, and the kids are all falling down the steps and crashing into each other as they try to get out of the way.

I run in the hallway and scream *"Security!!!"* and, miraculously, five police officers are in the room a moment later, but not soon enough to avoid a couple of kids getting punched in the "crossfire," among them David, one of my favorite students (he always takes attendance for me and helps me pass things out), who jumps between Bryant and Ian in an effort to break them up.

"No, David! Don't go in!" I yell, grabbing him by the back of the shirt as security floods the room. And then I leap up on the desk for visibility and yell, *"Everyone sit down and get out of the way! Now!!!"* Meanwhile, the dean has busted in yelling for everyone to get down, shut up, sit at their desks, etc., and they listen to him. There are kids falling all over each other, scrambling to get out of the middle of the fight and into their seats, or cramming up against the wall to let all the guards come through. Within moments, the fight is defused, the two culprits escorted out in handcuffs (because they wouldn't stop punching each other).

"David! Don't try to break up a fight like that ever again!" I yell, practically freaking out.

"Aww, Miss, he wouldn't have slugged me." (I'm not sure whether "he" refers to Ian or Bryant, and I'm definitely not convinced of his logic.) Meanwhile, security guards come into the classroom to interview various students, take statements from them, and at one point come in to take a poll from the students ("Now we really need you to tell the truth, kids," they say.) about who hit whom first. Although most of the kids want to stand up for Ian, when they're threatened with obstruction of justice they tell the truth: Ian actually touched Bryant first, although Bryant deserved it. We receive five separate visits by security during the first twenty minutes of class.

It is during one of these visits that the assistant principal of my department and his sidekick, the literacy coach, decide to come in and make surprise "walk-in" to my class!

"Um . . . we just had a fight," I tell them lamely.

"A fight?"

Then they see the security guard and say together, "Oh."

I kind of hope they'll take the hint to leave and come back another day, but they don't. Instead they tell me "Don't worry about it" (whatever that's supposed to mean) and make themselves comfortable. So I leap into teaching mode, praying that the kids will follow. I break them up into groups and have them finish working on some plays they were writing and then ask them to act them out. The literacy coach and the assistant principal wander around asking the kids questions about what they're doing, what kinds of things they're learning, etc. The kids are articulate and engaged.

"We acted white," they tell me later.

Argh.

CHAPTER SIX

Anita & the Sunshine Class

A nita was bold and brassy, with a big mouth. She had a wide smile that revealed perfectly straight rows of large, almost square white teeth, and she habitually screamed the latest gossip across the room, perfectly content for the entire class to be privy to her conversations.

"Volume control, Anita," I would tell her, motioning towards her with a calculator as though it were a TV remote.

"Don't be hatin', Miss," she'd holler back in a mock warning.

Her pink pen was an ongoing source of contention between us. It had a huge magenta feather sticking out the top and wrote in bright neon pink ink, her huge bubble letters scrawled on both sides of the page so as to make the entire thing illegible. Every time, I would write "BLUE OR BLACK PEN PLEASE!!!" in angry capitals all over her homework assignments. When I returned them to her, she would just laugh. I threatened to deduct points, a threat she correctly realized I would never make good on; her attendance record was spotty, her chance of passing the class was already in jeopardy. I wanted as many kids passing as possible.

"I'm going to go blind if you keep using that pen!" I told her. "It makes it so hard for me to read!"

"Miss! How you gonna be telling me not to write in pink? It's, like, my personality," she said, with exaggerated hand gestures.

I tried another tactic. "But I grade the papers in red pen. My corrections don't show up well against the pink."

"So grade me in green, Miss," she said with her usual pragmatism.

She and a group of other girls used to braid my hair after class, when I would let them. One afternoon they stayed afterwards, attempting to give me cornrows.

"Owwww!" The sensation of pulling on my scalp was excruciating. I didn't understand how the kids put up with this beauty regiment on a day-to-day basis.

"Quit crying, Miss! You're so tender-headed!" Anita laughed, as she yanked one of the braids and pulled as hard as she could. (At least, that's what it felt like to me—I couldn't tell what was happening behind my head.) One of the other girls squeezed my hand.

Later that night, I removed the few braids they had gotten in before I had donned a winter cap and run off in terror—they were just too painful. When I sheepishly entered class the next day, hair still wavy from the aborted braiding attempt, only Anita noticed. She looked up at me, smirked, and shook her head knowingly.

————

Anita's class, despite their ongoing interest in torturing me with the latest hair fashions, was not by any means my toughest group. This semester, a group that their exasperated teachers called "the Sunshine Class" had been dumped upon me.

The Sunshine Class was mostly male. It contained at least one kid who had been upstate in Ossining's juvenile center, several who reported to probation officers, and members of both the Bloods and a local Albanian gang known as ABI. With a couple of notable exceptions, they all coexisted in relative peace, but seemed collectively uninterested in obeying any school rules. Teaching them involved writing almost daily incident reports. One day I confiscated a switchblade that one of the kids showed off. A few days later, a graffiti marker. By October, I had added a bottle of *Dos Equis* that they were passing around to my collection of contraband.

"Miss! Are you going to drink that?" they asked me gleefully.

"Please—after every single one of you guys' germs are all over it? Nah, I think I'll pass," I said, pouring the contents down the sink. Our English class had a sink because we were in a science lab.

"Nooooo," they all groaned in unified anguish as the alcohol flowed down the drain.

The bottle's owner, Jesus—one of the kids to whose probation officer I would report every week—asked, "Are you going to tell Giordano?"

Giordano was the dean. He would storm into classrooms without knocking, write up any student who was wearing a do-rag for detention, and then slam the door on his way out. The kids hated him. The faculty didn't like him much more.

"I'm *supposed* to tell Giordano right away. But, I'm going to make you a deal. I'll keep this to myself," I paused and looked meaningfully at Jesus, and then up at the rest of them, "so long as not a single one of you ever brings alcohol into my class ever again. Because if you do, there will be consequences."

They looked somewhat abashed, and I thought I had gotten through. But the following week, Jesus was sitting in the back of the class drinking out of what looked like a bottle of Scope.

I went over and demanded that he hand me the bottle. He did. I sniffed it: vodka and what I assumed was green food coloring.

The kids were waiting in quiet anticipation to see if I would figure it out. I gave them an exasperated look. "Very creative," I said.

They all burst out laughing.

———

Anita found out that she was pregnant around Christmas. She came to me and told me when I was substituting for another class, which had only two students—typical for the days just prior to vacation.

I was slightly surprised that she had chosen to tell me. If I had been told to name the students with whom I was closest, she wouldn't have been one of them—we certainly liked each other well enough, but we had never talked intimately until this moment.

But now, here she was, sitting in front of me, crying. "How's he gonna be asking me 'How you know the baby's mine?'" she sobbed, referring to her nineteen-year-old boyfriend's request for paternity tests. "I know because he's the only man I've been with this entire year! And here he is acting like I'm sleeping around."

"So what did you say to him?" I asked, patting her hand.

"I told him, 'Fine, I'd rather have you *gone* than have you be around without wanting to be in the child's life,'" she said.

"Can you do this on your own?"

She shrugged and sniffled.

"Would you consider putting the baby up for adoption, or . . .?" I wasn't sure what was appropriate for me to suggest. Thus far, my master's program had offered nothing in the way of instruction that seemed remotely applicable to this situation.

"I'm Catholic—I can't have an abortion," she said with certainty, preempting the question I had been unable to articulate. That thought seemed to sober her somehow, and she wiped her nose. "Whatever, I'll figure something out."

I later noticed Anita talking to a girl named Zuleka, who I did not teach but had spoken to on several occasions. Zuleka was a teen parent herself—I had found out from another teacher that Zuleka was living in a group home that offered babysitting services so the young mothers could finish high school.

"Did Zuleka give you some good ideas?" I asked Anita later that day.

"Yeah—she's amazing. She gave me the number of her teen center and everything."

I felt hopeful that something would work out, but I kept my distance anyway—I did not know how much I was supposed to pry.

In the Sunshine class, there was a kid named Derrick. He was a heavy-set kid with huge fake diamonds in both ears and long eyelashes. He was also inexcusably stupid. It wasn't merely that he failed academically; he had a propensity for finding the toughest kid in any given classroom, repeatedly annoying this kid sufficiently so that fists would be about to fly, and then backing down the moment things reached fever pitch. Then the other students and I would be left trying to calm down a furious kid while Derrick cowered behind the sink in the science lab. This happened repeatedly over the time I taught him, both in my class and in other ones.

Then there was Tony, a kid who made me especially nervous which, in this class, was some feat. He had just been released from the youth center at Attica. He was smart—"All you could do when you were bored was read books up there," he once told me—but had an explosive temper. "Yo, just shut up, mothaf—ah!" he would yell at kids who were annoying him. Then he would glower at them. I never once saw a kid disobey him. His long hair was in one tight braid at the back of his head—it resembled the spine of a stegosaurus, I thought—and he would some-times wear sweat suits with pictures of handguns embossed in a colorful pattern all over them. He wasn't the type of kid you wanted to pick on.

Unless you were Derrick, of course.

"Yo. Those shoes are mad stupid," Derrick said to him one morning. Tony glanced up, saw that it was Derrick talking to him, and promptly went back to reading *To Kill a Mockingbird*.

Derrick was undeterred. The boys, Tony included, had recently taken to wearing pink polo shirts with matching pink laces, in an homage to prep school fashions that I couldn't help but find ironic. That said, I thought they looked handsome in their polos, and I told them that I was happy they were dressing so nicely for school. So Tony was by no means the only guy sporting pink—but he was the one Derrick had decided to start up with.

"Yeah, those white shoes with pink laces—they be mad gay!" he said pointedly.

Tony jumped out of his seat and swung around to face Derrick in the top of the amphitheater style seats.

"That's *it!*" he screamed. "That shit makes me *tight*, you stupid mothaf—ah! And I love being tight, because then I can whip your sorry ass! You know what? I'mma lay my homies on you, and we got bigger knives than you, and bigger guns than you! You dead, mothaf—ah! You dead, you hear me?"

He started towards Derrick. Jermaine, a relatively small boy, looked from Tony to Derrick, and immediately jumped out of his seat to try and stop the impending showdown, grabbing Tony by his arms from behind using a wrestling hold. He held on with all his might, even though Tony was thrashing towards Derrick.

Derrick, for his part, was sitting in his desk looking confused.

"Derrick!" I screamed, while pulling on Tony's shirt to help Jermaine, "Apologize to Tony! *Right now!*"

Derrick stared at us.

"*Say you're sorry, Derrick!*" I turned to Tony, and said "Tony! He's being an idiot! Just ignore him, okay?"

At this point, Tony shook himself, shrugging off Jermaine and me. But instead of hitting Derrick, he turned, walked down the amphitheater steps, and stormed out of the room, slamming the door behind him.

———

Meanwhile, in Anita's class, rumors of her condition spread. Though pregnancy was hardly unusual in their circles, the students still found it to be gossip worth repeating. Cooper, a slow basketball player whose stated aim in life was to pick up his average to a 65 so that he'd be eligible for the team again, decided it was fodder for class amusement.

"Yo, Miss, some people in this class be getting pregnant," he said loudly during group work, looking pointedly at Anita.

No one knew exactly what to say. Anita either ignored him or didn't hear, but a couple of kids snickered uneasily. Bolstered by their reaction, he added to this proclamation:

"Yeah, there's some sluts in this class, is all I'm saying."

At this, Anita stood so quickly that she knocked over a desk, reached over several desks, and smacked Cooper dead across the face. The smack made such a noise like out of a movie. It must have been painful.

Cooper stood in shock for a moment. Then he lost it.

"*You f—ing bitch!*"

"*F—you, you piece of shit! How you gonna be talkin' about my business like that in class?*"

"*Suck my dick, you stupid fat slut!*"

And they went at each other, kicking, punching, and screaming obscenities at the tops of their lungs. Cooper wasn't a huge guy and probably didn't outweigh Anita by that much; she was a formidable opponent for him, as for anyone else who tried to keep her from him. The other students and I found it relatively easy to pry Cooper off of Anita: "Get me away from that psycho bitch!" he yelled. But it was more difficult to get Anita to cease and desist: "F—ing asshole, I'll teach him to be getting up in my business in class!"

Just as the students and I had succeeded in separating them security burst in and cuffed both of them. "You have to calm down," one of the guards told Anita, who was screaming and thrashing in her cuffs as she was lead out the door. Cooper, for his part, just looked sheepish.

"He started it," I said lamely to one of the guards, as I wrote up a statement that tried to reflect Anita's ferocity in a light of justified indignation.

The guard looked at Cooper and rolled his eyes. "Yeah, we'll sort it out in mediation," he told me.

———

That same month, Derrick managed to piss off Jesus.

Perhaps the Sunshine Class's most charming and handsome member, Jesus had olive skin, brown eyes, and a dark brown Afro that he would spend hours combing to perfect fluffiness, usually in the middle of class. The girls liked him. The boys found his antics—particularly his ongoing efforts to sneak alcohol into the school in various creative ways—wildly entertaining.

Rules of any sort—school policies or laws—were irrelevant, as far as Jesus was concerned. Whenever he got in trouble, which was fairly often, he would always be far more interested in explaining to anyone who would listen (me, the deans, other students) what slipup on his part had caused him to "get caught." He never defended himself; he also never seemed concerned about punishments.

I don't remember what Derrick did, but whatever it was, it must have been particularly annoying, since Jesus never seemed to get upset. It was near the end of class, and suddenly Jesus was standing on the top tier of the amphitheater seats, holding the stool that usually sat behind the science table at the bottom. It was a three-foot-tall metal contraption, designed to not go up in flames (unlike the wooden desks) if the room were to combust from some gas explosion. Jesus held the stool high in the air, looking at Derrick with mild irritation. As I watched, he reached his arms back behind his head, stool still in hand, and prepared to launch.

"Jesus!" I cried. "Don't throw the stool! Please!"

Derrick stood across the room, mouth slightly agape.

Just then, the door opened and the next period class—a sweet but rowdy group of boys, half of whom were in the Special Education Inclusion program—came into the room, cheerfully oblivious to the standoff that was going on between Jesus and Derrick.

"Jesus. Come on. Do not throw the stool," I called to him from the doorway, where I was trying to hold back the next class from entering. Derrick, for his part, remained frozen.

Just then, the security guards—on time for once—came through the door. "Drop the stool, Jesus!" one of the guards said. In an instant, Jesus dropped the stool—it bounced down the amphitheater steps with loud clanking, knocking the desks off center. Jesus then sprinted to the window, opened it up, and jumped out. (In subsequent years, all the windows in the school were nailed so that they could only be opened about five inches, maximum—but back then, there was no such restriction.) We were only on the first floor, and there was a huge garbage canister outside, so it was an easy exit. I watched him run across the football field.

The guards grabbed Derrick and dragged him out of the room. "Call us if Jesus comes back," one of them said.

I started my lesson with the next class. Fifteen minutes later, the kids were doing group work, and Jesus climbed into my room again through the same window.

"Um, security's looking for you," I told him.

"Hmm . . . okay," he said, looking nonchalant. He walked calmly to the classroom door, left the room, and closed it softly behind him. The kids and I looked after him.

———

Whatever equivalent drama might have taken place in Anita's classroom after her historic showdown with Cooper was neatly thwarted by events beyond anyone's control. Anita came to me at the beginning of class a few days later looking flushed and panic-stricken.

"Miss, I gotta talk to you," she whispered.

"Can I take attendance first?"

"No . . . now!"

I walked her to the door, out of earshot of the other students. "Okay, what's up?"

"I'm bleeding."

She turned around and bent over a little bit, pointing for me to look. Sure enough, there was a tiny spot of blood pooling in the crotch of her jeans. She was having a miscarriage in the middle of my classroom. All things considered, she seemed calm. We looked at each other for a moment. And then, not knowing what else to do, I passed the buck—I sent her three doors down to the nurse. It was too late, and she lost the baby.

———

The assistant principal, or AP, came to observe my teaching of the Sunshine Class. Jesus decided this was prime time to open a pack of cigarettes, light one, and start smoking.

"Jesus, please put away the cigarettes," I said, hoping the AP would take notice of how difficult this class was. The AP looked up at Jesus, but said nothing—apparently part of my evaluation would be based on how I dealt with this situation.

Jesus looked curiously at me. Then he stubbed out the cigarette and stuffed it back into his pocket.

The AP pulled out what looked like a palm pilot. He then unfolded it, revealing a small, flat keyboard attached to it. He began to type on it.

"Cooool," the kids all said in unison. He ignored them.

I started my lesson again. Things were moving along at a good clip when the AP noticed that Derrick was not taking notes.

"Who is this student?" he asked. Then to Derrick he said, "Take out your notes."

"Suck my dick," Derrick responded.

The AP didn't seem to know how to handle this remark. He stared at Derrick, and then began furiously typing on his tiny keyboard. I made a mental note to kill Derrick if my evaluation was anything less than satisfactory.

Arben, a member of a local Albanian gang, was goofing around. I had seen him burn his own arm routinely with cigarettes; I also knew he had been to a court case earlier that year for hitting a member of a rival gang member over the head with a cinderblock. Compared to this, chatting with his neighbor during class seemed inoffensive.

The AP was unimpressed, however. "You. Come talk to me outside," he said to Arben.

"Who is this f—er?" Arben asked me, pointing a thumb at the AP.

"That's Mr. Vasilios—he's the assistant principal, Arben."

"What the f—'s he doing here?"

Somehow the AP managed to get Arben to leave the room with him. Moments later they were back. "Fag," Arben muttered under his breath. Either the AP didn't hear him, or he chose to ignore it.

After class, the AP informed me that I needed to do a better job instilling the importance of school rules in the students. "See, you saw how I took Arben outside and told him that we simply don't use profanity in this school," he pointed out. "You need to enforce discipline."

My observation report received a mark of "satisfactory."

––––––––––

"So I was supposed to take this pill, to make sure I didn't have a miscarriage," Anita explained to me in an offhanded manner when she returned the week after the in-class fiasco, "but I forgot to take it." I wondered about the medical validity of what she was saying, but refrained from asking. "But it's better that I'm not having the baby, anyway."

"Is that what you decided?" I asked her.

She looked embarrassed for a moment, and then said to me, "Miss, I didn't tell you, but that day when I talked with Zuleka and all that—well, I'd already told my mom about the pregnancy. And she told me if I had the baby she was going to kick me out of the house," she said. "So, it's good in a way that I lost the baby." She shrugged. Then she bounced off down the hallway to talk to her friends.

––––––––––

Jermaine was absent from the Sunshine Class for a week in the spring. His home phone line was disconnected, and calls to his parole officer went unanswered. Then one morning he returned, waltzing into class ten minutes before the end of the period. "*Yes!* There's still ten minutes left!" he cried joyfully. He sat down and took his pen and paper out of his bag, ready to work.

I asked him where he had been.

"Oh, I got picked up by the police, Miss," he told me. "They had me on breaking and entering, but I was . . . what do you call it . . ." He thought for a moment, and then his eyes brightened: "Falsely implicated!"

In keeping with the fashion of the Sunshine Class, he was wearing a neatly pressed dress shirt with bright pink stripes. The buttons at his wrists were undone.

"Can you help me with these?" he asked me, holding them up.

I buttoned them for him. When I looked up, I realized the boys were watching us, silently, in something like fascination.

"See Miss? We're not so bad. At least no one in our class got pregnant," one of them said. "And we didn't get anyone else pregnant either," someone else added. The others murmured in assent.

"You know, that's true. Good work guys," I said. I straightened Jermaine's collar for him. Then I picked up *To Kill a Mockingbird* and continued the day's lesson.

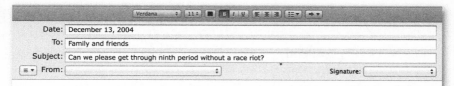

Date: December 13, 2004
To: Family and friends
Subject: Can we please get through ninth period without a race riot?
From: Signature:

I can only tell this the way it happened. Today, out of nowhere, a group of black girls—Kristina, Danielle, and Erica—in my eighth-period class announced, "Have you ever noticed how we're all black so we all stick together?" This should have warned me right off the bat that something was amiss, but I thought little of it. Then, when we were doing group work, they said, "You better put Silvana (who is Albanian) or Beba (who is Latina) with us, so they actually do work, because otherwise they just talk." Naturally, Beba, Silvana, and their crew were offended. I remixed the groups, putting Kevin and Danny, two boys, into the group with the black girls, but then they started calling Danny and Kevin "fat lazy asses" and everyone else "low class"—a clear reference, in these circles, to their cultural or economic backgrounds—and then none of the boys wanted to work with them either.

I think my first mistake was one of omission—I should have sent everyone out for mediation rather than allowing this to escalate. But instead I tried to reason with Kristina and Co. that it wasn't their business what kind of work anyone else was doing, and that they should stop being so incredibly rude and just start their work like I'd told them to. At this point, the black girls turned it on *me*, which caught me off guard—they said that I'm too "nice" with the class, and that no one does what they're supposed to because I don't "control them." This hit a nerve, because I am often concerned about being perceived as a pushover. And that was my second mistake—I shouldn't have let them engage me in any argument. Hindsight is 20/20, right? Instead, I tried to reason with the black girls and point out their rude behavior. They responded that they were just "speaking their minds," and that everyone else is "too white." During this time, other students were getting so offended they just got up and walked out.

Nothing got done. And I was so upset that I didn't know how things had spiraled so out of my control—I was just glad when the bell rang. A period later, the Albanian and Latina girls returned to the classroom, screaming. They were all scraped, bloodied, and black-eyed. I was told that the black girls accosted the Albanian and Latina girls in the stairwell, made some racial slurs at them, and then, when the Albanian and Latina girls wouldn't fight, accused them of being "pussies" and threatened to poke their eyes with pens. A fistfight ensued. One of the Albanian girls, Silvana, shouted hysterically, "We didn't do anything! They tried to push Beba down the stairs!" Everyone was crying, screaming, trying to get in his or her side of the story.

By this point, enough people knew about the fight that the Latina and Albanian girls were concerned about someone waiting outside the school to "jump" them. So while the school police took statements, I called all the parents to let them know what was going on. The parents, of course, went crazy with worry; one came to pick her child up in a cab, and another called me back, crying, asking why there wasn't better security in the school that would protect her child from being stabbed in the eye with pens. I had no good excuses to give her. I made several other calls, cleaned wounds, and finally left forty-five minutes late for my City College class.

And here's the icing on the cake. I opened my wallet to go buy coffee and found no money in it. I'd had $40 at lunch. During the scuffle, some student (I have a hunch that it's my resident sociopath, but that's just my suspicion) went into my purse, which I probably put down on the desk, and took out all my spare cash. And this, for me, was really hard to deal with. I had a hard time keeping from crying; I think it was more hurtful than anything else, because you want to believe that your students respect you enough not to steal from you. And even if you know that the resident sociopath is, in fact, a sociopath—and have seen him do things before that make you firmly believe it was he who did the stealing—you still can't help feeling backstabbed and betrayed because all you've wanted to do is teach him.

CHAPTER SEVEN

Chris

Chris was the scariest-looking kid in my entire ninth-grade class. At sixteen, he was a foot taller than me. He barely spoke or interacted with anyone, even when spoken to. Instead, he cast a narrow-eyed scowl around the room at all times. Sometimes he fixed his stare on me, and I would have the uncomfortable feeling that he was plotting against me. His eyebrows arched steeply, and his hair was made into hard, dry spikes with gel. From the conical metal stud in his ear, to the acute angle of his small goatee, everything about Chris seemed sharp.

I tried again and again to engage him in group work and class discussions; he would move his chair over to the group when I told him to, but then he would sit there doing nothing, much to his boisterous classmates' confusion.

Even the other kids found him menacing. "Yo, what's up with that guy?" one of the kids whispered to me after a futile attempt at engaging Chris in conversation. I shrugged.

Another one said to me in confidence, "Chris looks at you like he's gonna jump you after class!"

Initially I wondered if perhaps Chris was illiterate, or if English just wasn't his first language. A discussion with his former English teacher cleared up both these misconceptions—he spoke only English and could read as well as any of them. Still, he didn't do any homework and failed the first *Romeo and Juliet* test. Just when I was set on not liking him, citing his frustratingly indifferent attitude as a reason, something miraculous occurred.

It began with my thesis project for my education degree. My hypothesis was that students' behavior would improve when given the opportunity for reflective writing in class. To test this, I bought each student a pen and a brightly colored journal. This immediately led to fights, red and black being the most popular colors, but I remained undeterred. I instructed the students to do "journaling" (as it is called in our profession) during class, and every Friday I had them fill out a behavior survey tallying up how many disciplinary infractions they had had that week.

As it turned out, my students refused to take the journal time seriously, preferring to stick pencils, paper balls, and half-eaten candy bars—anything small—into an exposed, open vent in our classroom that had powerful suction force. The thrill of the day would be holding the test-item loose next to the vent, and then releasing it so that it went flying into the darkness. Then they would scream with joy and dance around. During the time that they spent doing the journaling project, they actually had *more* disciplinary infractions than ever before. The experiment was a complete failure.

Except for Chris.

For some reason, he really took to it. He wrote a journal entry every single day, scowling at the kids who dared disturb him. Every single one of his journals was about cars: building cars, fixing cars, different color cars, racing cars, cars he would own when he got older, etc. His writing consisted entirely of simple sentences and declarative statements: "My favorite car is a Mustang. I want it in black. When I graduate high school and get a job, I will buy a black Mustang." But it brimmed over with enthusiasm and tiny, detailed drawings of cars in the margins.

"Chris, this is just great!" I told him one day midsemester, sitting in the desk next to him and looking over his journal. The other kids, though they were supposed to be journaling, were stuffing junk into the vent again. "You're keeping a beautiful journal! I am so proud of you!"

"Huh-huh," he laughed, in a dead-on impersonation of Beavis and Butthead. I patted his head. His hair crunched.

Despite barely saying anything, doing any homework, or participating in class, Chris's near-perfect attendance and devoted journaling earned him a passing grade of 65 at the end of the first marking period. When I told him, he was clearly pleased—"Huh-huh, 65. That's hot." He let me give him a hug.

————

Thrilled as I was with my own pedagogical ability, it took me a while to notice the changes that were occurring in Chris—specifically, the changes to his eyebrows. Chris started coming into class with little lines shaved in them, from top to bottom. That's all they were—clean, thin little lines, where his skin was peeking through. First he had one little line. Then two. Then several.

"Chris! What the hell are you doing?" I asked him point blank, recognizing the eyebrow shavings as a gang identifier. I knew this from my extensive perusal of FBI gang websites.

He grinned. "Huh-huh. What?"

"Your eyebrows! The shave lines—you're joining a gang!" I said to him, and then I immediately backpedalled for fear of sounding too accusatory. "I mean, are you?"

"Huh-huh. No," he said, and grinned at me again.

"Oh." I blushed, flustered.

I dropped the subject, because I did not know how to proceed. It struck me that I was faced with a peculiar problem: There is no polite way to ask someone if they are in a gang.

A couple of weeks later, when I was marking the kids' journals after school, I saw that Chris has written the word "Bloods" in stylized gang lettering all over his little red notebook. I called him to my desk the next day.

"Chris, what is this about?" I asked him, pointing to one of the many "Bloods" insignias on his notebook.

"Huh-huh. Miss, that's my brother's gang. Not mine."

Oh, terrific, I thought. *Just what he needs—an older sibling to pull him in.* "Chris," I said. "I'm scared for you. The Bloods—they're not a joke. They kill people. They're really *f—ing* dangerous," I told him, enunciating the swear word so he knew I meant business. "Please, Chris. Don't get involved with them."

"Huh-huh. Miss, you cursed."

"I know. Look at me," I sighed, realizing the absurdity of myself—a small, white, female teacher in khakis, a striped polo shirt, and Harry Potter glasses—trying to impress upon Chris the dangers of gang activity. "Are you listening to what I'm telling you?"

"Yeah, Miss. Huh-huh," he said. But he would not meet my eyes.

It occurred to me that for all I felt that I'd connected with this kid through his journaling, I really don't know the first thing about his life outside of school. An image of a bigger version of Chris, with more facial hair and more menace, popped into my head: He was surrounded by tough-looking guys, all with arms folded aggressively, bandanas, tons of eyebrow shaving lines, and guns hooked into the waists of their baggy jeans. I had no idea if this was how a gang would really look—and realizing the potential inaccuracy of this image just underscored for me how far away I was from Chris—and how powerless I was to stop him from joining them.

Towards the end of the term, his attendance diminished alarmingly. I called his home but the phone line was disconnected. I made a note to the guidance counselors, but everything was chaotic with the approach of finals and Regents exams; whatever efforts were made on their part, Chris somehow got lost.

In the next semester, the students were reshuffled into new classes to break up "clusters" who would urge each other towards mischief. I ended up with some of the same ones again, but Chris was no longer on my roster. I looked around for him, thinking that I would run into him in the hallway at some point, but it didn't happen. When I asked after him, the kids look at me funny and said "Miss, he dropped out. . . . Didn't you know?"

———————

A month passed, in which I tried to make progress with my new students. This term, my room had no exposed vent for wasting candy and, to make it worse, I'd been assigned to teach three periods of English in a science lab again. Every day I would come in to find that the kids had turned the gas knobs to "on." They were constantly milling around up at the front, by my desk, asking, "What does this knob do? How about this one?" I had serious concerns that the room would explode.

One of my sections was a tenth-grade Inclusion class, wherein roughly half the kids were special education students. There were thirty-three of them, all boys. To compensate for my being twenty-three years old and female, I was assigned to team-teach with a middle-aged male special education teacher. Unfortunately, he spoke mostly Tagalog. He was kind and well-intentioned, but as everyone in the class spoke either English or Spanish, he was rather ineffectual. When the boys would act up, which happened constantly, the teacher would yell in thickly accented English, "Class! You stop that one right now!" This would cause them to burst out laughing, and then they would continue punching each other, throwing things, or freestyle rapping.

Truthfully, I often found them quite amusing, but nothing was getting done. When I complained to the principal about the unholy levels of testosterone, suggesting that perhaps the group should be reshuffled, she told me not to let my "sexist suppositions about boys override [my] objective view of the class."

Even the boys knew that an all-male class of thirty-three was not ideal: They kept complaining that it was "mad gay" and "a sausage fest."

Sometimes I would look at the all-boy class and think of Chris. I would ask myself if perhaps he would have done better in a big male group, where perhaps some bonding with the other guys might have kept him occupied with their brand of goofy behavior rather than big-time trouble. It was hard not to wonder about him.

One sunny Tuesday afternoon, the bell had just rung to begin sixth period. I was in the process of settling the kids down, giving the usual instructions to stop touching the gas knobs, to go sit down, and to take out a paper and writing implement. Danny, a little guy with curls sticking out of his contraband do-rag, asked, "Miss, can I go to the bath-room?"

"Yes, but hurry. You don't want to miss anything."

He left, and then a second later reentered the room.

"I thought you were going to the bathroom," I told him.

"Miss, they said I'm not allowed to go . . . there's a fire drill."

"A fire drill," I repeated, looking at him for clarification. Gener-ally, the teachers were sent memos about fire drills in advance. At that moment, an announcement came over the PA system telling everyone to evacuate for an "unplanned drill." I told the kids to gather their stuff, and we made our way outside.

The sidewalks around the school looked like New Year's Eve in Times Square. Kids were packed ten-deep, and a fire truck, along with several extra squad cars (beyond those of the NYPD unit that was permanently based in our school) were parked around the building. Police and fire department presence was not unusual for a fire drill, and we paid no heed. Within seconds, I had lost nearly all of my students in the crowd, but it did not matter. We were all so elated to be out of the classrooms on a beautiful day.

Thirty minutes passed before I realized that we'd been out here much longer than the length of an ordinary fire drill.

"Yo, what kind of fire drill is this? It's taking mad long!" said one of the kids.

I suspected a bomb threat. That was the only explanation I could think of for why this drill would be "unplanned," and why we'd be out here for thirty minutes with no instruction. As if reading my mind, several police officers began walking around, telling everyone to back away from the building. The mob retreated, so much so that we were relocated a block from the exit by which we had left.

A girl standing in a little group near me, whom I did not know, suddenly asked me, "Miss, you think it's a bomb?"

"It may be a bomb threat. But it's not real," I said hastily, looking at some of the students standing around us who appeared alarmed. "It's probably just some guy who wanted to spring his girlfriend from class so that they can go see a movie."

The kids giggled.

"Can we go get a slice of pizza, Miss?" they asked.

"I didn't hear you say that . . . so I absolutely would not know if you were cutting class," I told them, covering my ears in an exaggerated gesture of "hear no evil." They laughed. They were not even my students, so who was I to stop them? Especially since there was no sign of us being let back into the building anytime soon.

"We'll bring you one, Miss," they said. "What do you like on your pizza?"

"Uh . . . well, hypothetically, mushrooms."

Feeling irresponsible, I watched them as they went around the block and out of my field of vision. I expected that I would not see them for the rest of the day. But twenty minutes later they reappeared, pizza in hand. They even brought me a mushroom slice. Everyone was still standing outside.

An hour and a quarter into our evacuation, the doors opened, and we prepared to return to class. But the lines through the entrances were not moving. We realized that they were rescanning all three thousand students upon entry into the building, although at least one thousand of them had probably gone home.

"Nooo, what is this shit? How are they gonna scan everyone in again? By the time we get through, school will be done," the kids complained.

Sure enough, when we finally all got through, it was the beginning of eighth period, and only a few of my students remained. The mood in the school was tense. If anything, there were more cops than before.

They were all walking around the building mumbling into walkie-talkies.

Immediately after an announcement came over the PA saying that all lockers would be clipped that afternoon, the students surrounded my desk. "What's going on, Miss?" the kids asked me, while I took attendance. "Come on. Don't they tell the teachers what's happening?" They look imploringly at me.

"I know as much as you guys do," I told them, palms outstretched in front of me, showing I had nothing to hide. "Come on, let's get moving. Take out your memoirs."

We got working, and then there was a knock at the door. Several police officers looked into the classroom. They consulted a list. "Can we see . . . Muhammad Sulemane?" they asked, looking around the room.

Muhammad, an earnest kid with thick glasses and a buzz cut, looked nervous. He has probably never been in trouble before, I thought. He reluctantly rose from his seat.

"Bring your backpack with you," the cops told him sternly.

They ushered him outside the room, and we all looked at each other. I made a half-hearted attempt to start the lesson again. Less than a minute later, Muhammad came back in, unescorted, stuffing his gym clothes back into his backpack and looking irritated.

"Miss, they searched my stuff for no reason!" he fumed. "Isn't that racial profiling?"

———

Here is what I learned later: Sometime between 9:07 a.m. and 9:47 a.m., a student had entered the building with a handgun in his or her backpack and had then had the stupidity to put his backpack on the scanner. The scanner had picked up the image of a gun. The guards had been unable to figure out which backpack it was in. The administration had been trying to find it ever since.

———

Between the zaniness of my all-boy class and the action-packed thrill-ride that was our typical school day, I had all but forgotten Chris. So I was very surprised when one sunny day, while I was falling asleep on the 2 train on the way home from the school, the doors opened and Chris got on. He was in need of a shave, and there were tired rings under his eyes, though he seemed alert; his eyes darted furtively around the train car before he spotted me and smiled. The conical piercings and spiky hair remained unchanged.

"Miss! You remember me?" he asked.

"Chris! Of course I remember you. How are you doing, sweetheart?" We hugged. The people on the subway glanced at us curiously.

"Huh-huh. I'm okay. My mom's kicked me out, so now I live with my girlfriend at Jackson Avenue," he told me. It was the longest sentence he had ever uttered in my presence.

"What? Why did she kick you out?"

"Because I wanted to apply to, like, a trade school—for cars, Miss—and she wouldn't sign the forms."

"So, you mean, then you left?"

"No, then I got mad at her, and she hit me and told me to get lost, and then I left."

"Chris, that's awful. I'm really sorry to hear that," I said. Then, "Do you think there's any chance we might see you back at school sometime soon?"

He looked away. "Ugh, I don't know, Miss."

"Awww, Chris, why?" I implored and instantly hated myself for whining.

"Like, I'm having some trouble with the Bloods, Miss."

"Chris, please come to school. People can help you with that—you know Dean Markson, with that club he does for ex-gang members? The Council for Unity?" (The Council for Unity was a gang prevention program that one of the deans had started the previous year.)

He looked at me warily. "Miss, it's not like that." He looked around again, then leaned over and whispered in a low voice, "You know those parking lots . . ." He named two cross-streets in the South Bronx that I hadn't heard of.

"Chris, I'm not sure . . ."

He interrupted me, still whispering, "So there's these two guys who got killed there . . . and my brother was involved."

My stomach seemed to flip. "Chris, don't tell me this, please," I said, putting my hands over my ears. "I don't want to have to join the Witness Protection Program!"

"Huh-huh. Chill, Miss, it's cool," he said. For a moment I was worried I had offended him, but then I saw that he was grinning again.

A little while passed without either of us saying anything. The train trundled on southward.

"Chris," I finally said, "Did you know that someone actually brought a gun into the building a while ago?"

"Huh-huh," Chris chuckled. "You mean, that time everyone got let out?"

"Yeah. How did you know about that?"

"Miss, there's lots of guns that get in that building." He looked bemused.

"Lots of guns? Chris—what do you mean?"

"Kids sneak 'em in!" He said. He was now smiling broadly.

"How?" I asked, my voice rising to fever pitch. "Tell me how they're doing that!"

"Huh-huh. Miss, chill. It's easy—if you wrap the gun in electrical tape, then wrap it in, like, a gym shirt, and then stick it in the bottom of your bag under mad books and shit—then it won't go off on the scanner!"

I ran this information through my head. It didn't explain how the one gun I knew about had gotten into the school, as the scanners had picked that one up just fine—but I let it slide.

"So, how many guns do you think have gotten into the building in the last couple of months or so?" I asked him recklessly.

"I don't know—four? Maybe five?"

I opened my mouth, and then closed it again. I was stunned. Finally, I said, "Chris, would it be okay with you—like, you wouldn't get in trouble or anything—if I tell security what you just told me about the electrical tape?"

He thought about it for a few seconds. "Yeah, sure, just don't tell 'em I told you," he finally said. Then he realized we were at Jackson Avenue. "Oh, Miss, this is my stop. I gotta go!"

He stood, and I stood, too. I stole another quick hug.

"Please come back sometime soon," I told him.

Chris was already out the door, but he turned and smiled.

———

That week, I ambushed the dean of security in his office and regaled him with my newly acquired knowledge of gun-sneaking protocol. He humored me for a few minutes, and then told me he'd look into it, before rushing off to break up a fight. During the remainder of that year, a slew of other weird instruments were brought in and used as weapons, but I never heard of another gun on the premises.

All the while, I kept hoping to run into Chris whenever I was taking the train back into the city from the Northeast Bronx. I would look for him at the Jackson Avenue stop before the train went into the tunnel.

I told myself maybe he got his black Mustang and left the city for good.

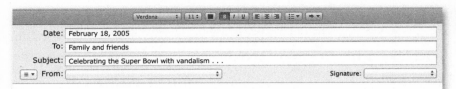

Date: February 18, 2005

To: Family and friends

Subject: Celebrating the Super Bowl with vandalism . . .

From: Signature:

During my first week teaching the thirty-three-person, all male, Special Education Inclusion kids class, the Super Bowl incited such a fervor that an Eagles fan got his jacket vandalized. Specifically, the word "Patriots" (the rival team) was written all over his jacket in permanent marker, except that it was spelled "Patroits." The poor kid was incredibly upset. "Miss, I paid for this jacket. I don't do anything to them. Why do they do this to me?" he asked. It would be bad enough without the fact that this kid is a Special Education student, and this is his first inclusion experience. I was ready to bust some tenth-grade rear end, but security beat me to it. They came bursting into the class and hauled out six kids who were allegedly responsible for the vandalism. I didn't even get to make the call.

However, one of the kids who was hauled out apparently decided it was my fault that he was blamed for the stupid incident. "Yo, Miss, I got two days suspension 'cause of you," he said menacingly in the stairwell. "I got somethin' for you in class." This kid is just barely five-feet, and your usual gangly fifteen-year-old. So I said, "Hey, guess what? I've got something for you, as well!" and slapped him with two more days of suspension for threatening a teacher. Then I called in his father, and we all had a meeting in which his father threatened to "have problems with him" if he didn't start behaving better. I was like, "Great, this kid's dad is Mr. Tough Guy on him!" As they were walking out, the kid says, "Hey Dad, I need a hundred dollars." Uh-huh. So much for Mr. Tough Guy. But the kid has behaved better since, so maybe something was accomplished.

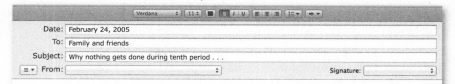

The thirty-three-boy class keeps fighting all the time. Mostly it's play fighting, but it's a little disconcerting when they keep ending up upside-down with their shirts off, heads in each other's laps. I'm serious. For some reason, beating each other up has to involve pulling your victim's shirt over his head and flipping him completely upside-down over your knees. I'm not even going to guess on this. I keep turning around and see them all piled up in the corner half naked, and I'm thinking, "Oh, good grief." Then they say, "Chill, we're just playing, Miss!" and laugh hysterically.

Most of the time their fighting is during tenth-period advisory (which is like study hall), by which point they're exhausted and wild and the special education teacher isn't with them anymore because it's not an academic course. I bought them all journals, markers, and pens to use during advisory. I said they could decorate whatever they wanted as long as they didn't decorate each other or each other's property. It sort of interests them, and they can sometimes spend quite a while drawing intricate gang symbols all over their journals. Problems begin when they throw the markers (always behind my back), and then it ends up being a full-scale war where they start jumping off the desks and tackling each other against the chalkboard.

Some teacher made the mistake of leaving a VCR in the room after her class period ended, so it was still there when my group came in. At the end of my class, once the bell rang and everyone left, these three kids started walking out of the room with the VCR, a mischievous glint in their eyes. I yelled, "Guys! Don't steal the VCR!" which of course sent them into gales of laughter, although, thankfully, they returned it and became preoccupied hitting me up for chewing gum and bus fare.

In English class, I wish they liked *To Kill a Mockingbird* better. They don't understand irony at all, and so most of the subtle humor of the book is lost on them. Plus, they don't get the distinction (despite my having explained it every way I could think of) between a book being "racist" and a book dealing with characters that are racist. So every time the word

"Negro" comes up, they say, "Oh my god! This book is racist!" and start throwing it across the room and talking of book-burnings and it takes forever to calm them down. I suspect there's a certain element of trying to get my goat here; with this crowd, I'm never quite sure if I've just set myself up to be the straight man.

CHAPTER EIGHT

Jonah

"You can't go in there," the female security guard said. Her voice was tinged with irritation at the argument she no doubt expected. She stood, blocking the doorway to stairwell 11, arms outstretched to prevent me from passing.

"Wasn't planning on it," I told her. I'd seen what I wanted to. Behind her, there was a visible spattering of blood—some still running down the walls, most pooled on the floor. I briefly considered that it didn't look like enough blood for someone to be dead—but then again, what did I know about these things? I turned and walked off, ignoring the irritation of the guard, as well as the slew of NYPD officers who were wandering the hallways talking in monotones on their walkie-talkies.

In high schools, there are no secrets. Everyone knew within the hour. A Bloods member had stabbed a DDP member with an ice pick.

This was a declaration of war. Bloods versus DDP. Bones, Crips, and Latin Kings were no doubt waiting on the sidelines, watching to see who would fall, and what alliances could be made or broken from this. Vito Corleone himself couldn't have imagined a more involved turf war.

"Wait a minute. Their gang is really called DDP?" I asked the kids.

"It stands for 'Dominicans Don't Play,'" they said.

"What?!?! That's the stupidest gang name I ever heard! I could make up a better gang name than that," I told them.

A few of them looked nervous. "Don't say that, Miss."

Whatever—I knew all the gang members in my class. There were no DDPs in here.

"Okay, so I have a new gang I'm starting. And it's just for teachers. It's called 'Teachas Don't Play': TDP. What do you guys think of that?"

Groans of "Yo, that's mad corny," and "Miss, why you beastin'?" filled the room.

I looked towards the back of the room, where Jonah Tejado sat. He smiled at me. Or, more accurately, he smirked. I don't think I ever saw him smile all the way. He was about sixteen and already a high-ranking member of the Bloods—not quite an O.G. (or Original Gangsta) yet, but he certainly had several stars. Black was the new color for the Bloods, because red had been banned as the catalyst for too many hallway fights. Jonah sported his black t-shirt oversized, with his pants hanging down past his boxers. A red bandana was just visible sticking out of his pocket. This was intentional.

"You got anything to add?" I asked him.

"Nah." He grinned. I liked Jonah. He didn't show up all that often, and rarely turned in homework, but he was smart and analytical. I knew he read on his own. Also, when the kids were acting crazy, he'd inevitably get sick of it and yell, "Yo, shut up n—s! Let her teach!" Out of either respect or fear—I wasn't sure which—they always did exactly as he asked.

"Does your mom know you're in a gang?" I'd asked him once, while the other kids were occupied with group work.

"No Miss, and don't tell her—she'll kick me out if she finds out."

So we had Jonah, Bloods rising star, sitting in our classroom. And the latest battle in an ongoing rivalry with DDP was taking place outside. Most of the fighting was off school grounds, but there was certainly a lot of orchestration when the guards weren't looking.

These random kids, some of them gang members, not all actually enrolled in our school, would sneak in through the back entrances, which were supposed to be guarded at all times, but patently were not, despite the extra security forces and metal detectors at the four main doors. It was hard to identify interlopers, since the school was so large, it was impossible to know every kid by face. But gang members had signs, if you knew what to look for: The telltale handkerchief hanging out of the pocket. Colored bead necklaces in intricate patterns that the kids told me had some gang meaning.

Naturally, security was oblivious to this. Or maybe they just had bigger things to worry about.

We were sitting in class a couple of days after the ice-pick incident when we noticed some kids in hoods at the doorway. They were looking into our class, clearly checking to see if someone was there. One of them pointed towards the back.

Jonah.

He seemed to be maintaining his composure. He stared them down. After a minute they left.

"Jonah, who were they?" I asked after class. But I already knew the answer.

"DDP, Miss."

"Are they looking for you?"

"Yeah. Whatever. It's fine."

Of course, they came back. Over the next couple of weeks, there were several incidents wherein someone looked through the window of our classroom door with interest, their gaze generally settling on Jonah.

I started locking the door after the kids came in.

"What do they want with you, Jonah?" I asked him. He looked at me and said, "You know." And he wouldn't elaborate.

To say the situation was making me nervous was putting it mildly. I'd told security I wanted someone stationed outside my classroom door. They always swore they'd put someone there, and yet somehow, I could never find a single guard when I needed one. And without an overtly violent incident, it was hard to make a case that such a presence was needed.

But the kids and I all knew what was going on. One way or another, the turf war was headed for our classroom door. Jonah's already spotty attendance record started developing gaping holes.

They came again. The visitors stopped outside our door, looking in with their usual combination of interest and malevolence. I wasn't sure if they were trying to communicate some sort of message to Jonah—something like, "You're f—ed—meet us after class in the parking lot," or if they were just trying to keep tabs on him.

Whatever it was, the class fell silent. I tried feebly to ignore the figures at the doorway and engage the students' interest in *To Kill a Mockingbird*, but it was to no avail. I thought about confronting them then and there, but I didn't. I was stuck on something that had happened to me in the previous year—something which, in retrospect, I'd often (incorrectly) conflated with this incident. It took me a while to understand why.

––––––––

It was my first semester of teaching ninth grade. The kids were working collaboratively. I was in the back of the room, bent over the joined desks of some students, when the room fell silent. I looked up to see a hooded figure—male, definitely—standing in the front of my classroom. Because of the way his head was angled, I couldn't see any of his facial features. He wore a black-hooded sweatshirt, which shadowed most of his face, and a pair of baggy jeans. He was taller than I was.

"Who are you? What are you doing here?" I asked him.

He didn't answer, but slowly gazed around the room, slamming is fist rhythmically into his palm. *Smack. Smack.* I gathered that he was looking for someone, though I had no idea whom. Casting a quick glance at my students' faces, I could tell they were confused, as well.

"Give me your ID," I said to him. I still couldn't see his face.

"F— off," he growled.

"What! Give me your ID! Now!"

The intruder ignored me. He turned and headed for the door. Mortified at having lost face in front of the ninth-graders by allowing a student to disobey me, I jumped in front of him and blocked the doorway with my body, trying to block his exit. He shoved me out of the way, knocking me against the doorway hard enough to leave a bruise. In desperation, I grabbed his sweatshirt, but he tore free and ran into the stairwell. He headed down.

I sprinted after him. I was furious and embarrassed; it seemed imperative to catch him. Looking back, I have no idea what I would have done if I had caught him, but I doubt that occurred to me at the time. I was heading down my third flight of stairs when I heard my ninth-graders above me yell, "Miss! Come back! Don't go after him! He's Bloods!"

I stopped in my tracks. I knew I had no hope of catching him anyway—I could no longer even hear the clump of his steps on the stairwell. Defeated, I headed back upstairs. I was crying, though I couldn't have said exactly why.

"Miss, it's okay to cry," the kids said when I reentered the classroom. My clothes were wrinkled, and I was sweating. They handed me tissues, and patted me on the shoulders uncertainly. One boy, Carlos, put his arm around my shoulder.

"I'm not crying, I'm just pissed off," I snarled, as I wiped my eyes.

Later, when security came in, the students offered that the intruder had been either black or Hispanic, wearing a hooded sweatshirt, and "mad gangsta." When pressed for further information, including how they had known he was "Bloods," they fell silent, nervously picking at their desks.

And I think that was what freaked me out the most. It was not just the loss of power, my obvious lack of meaningful authority; it was the fact that, whether due to loyalty or fear, the kids wouldn't give up the name of a dangerous intruder. And no matter how close I felt to them, ultimately I was alone.

———

So when the intruders were coming to Jonah's and my class, I remembered this incident. I suppose it would be accurate to say that I felt as though it was not Jonah, or the Bloods, but I who was having a turf war with DDP. I was angry, frustrated, and a little scared, but I had learned my lesson the first time. I wasn't going after them.

But by some act of fate, the problem solved itself. Perhaps the involved parties worked out their differences off school grounds; whatever the reason, the hoodlums did not return, at least not in a fashion that was apparent from the inside of my classroom. In a non sequitur that no one understood, it was not ice picks, but CD players that were banned by security after the fact.

Jonah came to class less and less often, and eventually failed, though not for lack of intelligence. I worried about him being jumped or shot outside of my classroom, but in the end, it was not Jonah, but Joel, one of the Crips, who took a bullet. Two actually. One grazed his head, and another grazed his pelvis, but he survived, and reemerged a couple of months later, with a cane and a lot of bravado to show for it.

I wondered who it was who shot him, and if perhaps the Bloods, or even Jonah, were involved. You never knew when the alliances might suddenly shift on you.

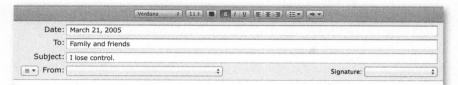

Date: March 21, 2005
To: Family and friends
Subject: I lose control.
From: Signature:

I think I have a tendency to mainly write emails when I've processed things and can sort of make neat little tales out of them. Here, I'm utterly bewildered. I lost it in front of my class today, and I really have no idea how everything got so out of control.

From the time they came in to the end of the ninety-minute double period, all they were interested in doing was arguing with one another. I tried so many times to teach the lesson, but I couldn't talk over everyone, so I eventually gave up and tried to wait them out silently, which usually works—only today, it didn't. It seemed like they were all way too interested in throwing each other's notebooks and calling each other vulgar names. The fighting had no apparent cause or reason. . . . Basically, it was just thirty kids screaming at each other for an hour. Occasionally one of them would start yelling at the others to be quiet, but it was usually done in such a condescending fashion that it resulted in the kid trying to police everyone becoming the newly attacked person. They just wouldn't stop.

I sent out four kids. I moved people around. I changed the lesson. I called in a dean. I waited silently again and again. Nothing worked. Eventually, as these events sometimes do when the kids get sick of arguing amongst themselves (mostly because they realize I'm not about to jump in), it turned into an attack on me: "Why would you want to teach high school if you can't control the class?" I retorted, "Because this kind of behavior has no place in a high school. No teacher would expect such immaturity in a tenth-grade class. . . . I signed up for high school so I could *teach* . . . not babysit." (This was followed by cheers of "Oooh! Smackdown!" while the girl who made the comment got up and stormed furiously out of the room.)

So this went on for about an hour more, and eventually I gave up waiting on them and trying to answer their snaps and did something I never do: I screamed at them. The reason I never do this is because it inevitably leads to me breaking down and crying. In my nearly two-year career, I have never until today broken down in front of a class (Although they tell you that you can't consider yourself a veteran teacher unless it's happened at least once, because it's *everyone's* worst nightmare.) And so here I am, sitting in front of thirty kids, just sobbing. "I just don't know what to do with you guys," I told them. "I'm here, trying every which way to teach you, prepare you for Regents, whatever, and you just don't want to listen. And I can't scream over you, and I can't fight you, and I can't scare you. What exactly do you want me to do here? I may not be your favorite teacher, and this may not be your favorite class, but I believe I am a good teacher and you could learn a lot from me . . . and then I see you wasting time like this, screaming and calling each other names and challenging me and throwing each other's stuff . . . and I don't know what to do. It just fills me with sadness and hopelessness."

I think they were stunned. Several kids apologized off the bat, a couple of the boys ran up and hugged me, some of the girls started crying, and then of course a few of them acted like total losers and just laughed. I guess I didn't have the heart to care much anymore. . . . I just felt tired and dazed. I wrote the assignment on the board, told them anyone who cared could muddle through it, but that really it was up to them to write it down; I wasn't going to get down their throats about it. I had nothing left in me.

I did, however, manage to call all of their parents, which was somewhat of a panacea for me. Plus, as I told them, they have a special guest tomorrow! They don't know it's the dean. They're in for a rude surprise.

Date: June 23, 2005
To: Family and friends
Subject: New school, new beginning?
From: Signature:

I was "excessed"—meaning my position was eliminated—from Explorers yesterday afternoon, for budgetary reasons and my lack of seniority in the system. I was hired before noon today by a small school in the building.[2] I accepted because they're giving me a really sweet program: for this coming semester, I have three classes of eleventh-grade English, a study hall and an elective of my choosing, a course I will call "Creative Nonfiction and the Personal Narrative."

The only downside is I still have my horrendous commute (and my schedule is early—7:40 a.m. to 2:15 p.m.!), but they have all kinds of grants for resources and computers and trips and things, so it should be a significantly different experience than teaching at Explorers proper. I don't know . . . I've been negative towards small schools because I see how bad it is for them to be in the same building as the larger school (in terms of using up resources and crunching the big school), but it seems that all big schools are headed to become small schools, anyway, whether I like it or not. And first and foremost I like being employed, and you don't knock the hand that feeds you.

The teachers who work at this new school say it's a really great place to work, that everyone's friendly and organized and easy-going. In fact, the lead teacher of the department is one of the girls with whom I've taken classes all the way through City College in the Fellows program, and we're very close, so it'll be great working with her. And I'll still be in the same building as all my Explorers friends, who promise not to shun me despite my having gone over to the "dark side." So I think, in the end, this may be a good change for me.

---

2   Since the early 2000s, formerly huge public schools around New York City have been gradually broken up into "small schools," all of which are housed in one building. On our campus, as many as seven schools have existed in the same building simultaneously, each with a separate administration. Often, the original "big school" is gradually phased out, while increasing numbers of small schools begin cropping up in its place. The result is acrimony between the different schools and an ongoing fight for space, resources, top teaching talent, and academic recognition.

YEAR 3

Date:	September 24, 2005
To:	Family, friends, and enemies
Subject:	Adventures in small schools and in mathematics . . .
From:	

Having long voiced objections to small schools on the grounds that they mooch off the existing big school's resources and spend a greater amount of money per student in a way that is unfair if the system can't afford to do so for every kid, I do feel somewhat like a turncoat at this point. That said, the working environment is much more agreeable. For starters, I have my own room, and a lot of leeway about what books I teach: In eleventh-grade English, for instance, I am teaching *To Kill a Mockingbird*, *Night*, and *The Bluest Eye* just because I like them, and not because of what was available in the book room. I am also teaching an elective I made up called Creative Non-Fiction and the Personal Essay, and a study hall period for which the tentative title is Shut Up and Do Your Homework or You have Lunch Detention. For the elective and study hall, I team-teach with the history teacher on the grounds that there are about a billion kids in the class at once. I told him I'd do the teaching and he could impose martial law. So far it's worked out fine.

This stupendous program couldn't last long, though, even in a well-run school. Apparently the kids have already managed to drive two of their teachers out with their bad behavior. One, they consistently taunted about her accent (and, allegedly, threw a stapler in the general direction of her head) to the point where she felt uncomfortable addressing the class. The other was openly gay, and though he cites "health reasons" as his impetus for leaving, common belief amongst the staff is that he left due to intolerance and resulting disobedience on the part of the freshmen. So the school was left scrambling to fill several spots this week. I received a knock at my door early Friday morning.

"I heard a nasty rumor about you," said the principal.

"Oh yeah, what is that?" I asked, worrying that he was going to chide me for lateness.

"I heard you can teach math."

"Um . . . I barely passed calculus."

"What? You don't need calculus to teach freshman math. You have the requisite number of credits. Please, we're desperate."

So now, in addition to my already existing course load, I am teaching ninth-grade math. This week I have to teach them about "box and whisker" graphs, which apparently are intended to give a visual representation of a set of integers. I never learned this in school (I feel like they just invented this kind of "new math" recently) and so I kind of want to call it a "bells and whistles" graph and march into class blowing a kazoo.

CHAPTER NINE

Adam

It felt like a first date.

During a school-wide faculty meeting the previous June, the assistant principal had pulled me aside.

"I have some bad news," he told me quietly, glancing around to make sure no one else could hear. "There were some last-minute budget cuts, which meant we couldn't afford to keep all the teaching positions . . . and so we had to excess some people. And it goes by seniority . . . so . . ."

I grabbed his forearm. "*What? You're firing me?*"

My eyes began to well up, but the vice principal said, "No, no! Don't cry! I didn't forget to take care of my girl!"

"You didn't?" I sniffed, while privately thinking, *That's a first.*

"No. The small school upstairs is looking for a new English teacher. I told them I'd send you up as soon as I talked to you."

I was interviewed that very day and hired the next. Within twenty-four hours, I had a new job. As I cleaned out my locker, it dawned on me how lucky I was to have been given an eleventh-hour reprieve from unemployment—surely other excessed teachers throughout the city had endured worse troubles.

But now, on my first day in the small school, I was shaking with nervousness. Supposedly, these kids were more studious than the ones in the main school—at the time, small schools could select their own students based on performance in middle school, cap their class sizes at seventy-five, and attendance average was close to 80 percent. By comparison, I was used to hundreds of students per grade in the main school, with attendance at closer to 50 percent. *Most of these kids will actually show up*, I realized. I had never had a class with decent attendance, and somehow, the prospect of having a full house each day was daunting.

I wiped my clammy hands on my blazer, an item I had never worn in the main school, and smoothed my hair. I had to make a good impression.

A boy and a girl walked into the class. Adam and Tonya, they told me. Juniors. I would be teaching them.

Neither looked big enough to be in eleventh grade, I thought. Adam couldn't have been more than my height of five feet, five inches—for a sixteen-year-old boy, that seemed quite small. He had a shorn head and a baby face. Tonya was probably under five feet, made only slightly taller by her platform shoes. She was rail thin, with her hair in cornrows so tight they looked painful.

"Whore," Tonya suddenly said to Adam, seemingly without provocation.

"Slut," he returned. I stared open-mouthed. Then they collapsed into giggles and hugged each other. Apparently this was an in-joke.

I introduced myself, and then started babbling awkwardly about whether I had bought enough pens for everyone. Adam, sensing my distress, reached out and hugged me. It surprised me how grateful I was.

"Don't worry, Miss," he said. "We're all a big family here. You'll be fine."

In class that day, I gave the students index cards and told them to write something on the cards that they felt I should know about them. Then people who wanted to share could read their cards aloud.

"What do we write?" the kids wanted to know.

"Anything," I told them. "You can write about what you did this summer. Or, if . . . say . . . you love reading—or, if you hate reading—you can tell me about that." I paused. "Or, you could just tell me about your hot new girlfriend or boyfriend."

The class giggled. When it was time to share, Adam's hand shot up, his neatly pressed little dress shirt only slightly rumpled from the day's affairs. I called on him.

"My name is Adam. I love reading. I do not have a hot new boyfriend, though I certainly wish I did," he read off his card, matter-of-factly.

Interesting, I thought. I had not realized Adam was gay until that moment. Not one of his classmates batted an eyelash. I thought, fleetingly, that he had them very well-trained; in the big school, any mention of being gay would have caused the class to erupt into screaming, with the boys all yelling "No homo!" as if this would ward off any suspicion of same-sex interest on their parts.

I had only had one openly gay male student before. He had insisted on being called "Cookie," which I found difficult to do without cringing. His classroom behavior had been so problematic that it pushed to the backseat any attempts to discuss with him the struggles he was undoubtedly going through being a gay teen in that school. Mostly, he had enjoyed instigating fights between people by writing gossipy notes, throwing things, and making public offers of sexual favors to the boys in our class, much to their horror. He got away with it because he was bigger than any of them.

I could tell that Adam was different.

"Adam is gay, right?" I asked one of the other teachers, just to make sure. I'd been off before—it seemed safer to verify in case I had somehow misunderstood.

She laughed and said, "As the day is long. He came out last year, in a grade-wide assembly. . . . He just got up on the stage in the auditorium and said, 'I have an announcement: I'm gay.'" She chuckled, remembering. "Actually, the kids were remarkably cool about it, considering."

I'm certain that Adam would have stuck out even if he hadn't been openly gay in the Bronx public schools. He wore light blue or periwinkle dress shirts and gray slacks to school, no matter what day it was. He carried a day planner everywhere he went. He spoke both English and Spanish with near perfect elocution. He was one of those kids you immediately identify as a teacher's pet, but somehow, he pulled it off without seeming saccharine or disingenuous.

"Miss? Can you help me with my math homework?" asked Callum, one of the eleventh-graders. It was study hall during the first week of school, when everyone was still keeping up the pretense of using that time to do homework.

"Sure . . . what're you guys learning about?" I walked over to his desk and looked down at his homework. "My mortal enemy. Logarithms . . . we meet again."

Callum burst out laughing. "Miss, it's okay—I'll ask Adam." He turned and yelled across the room, "Hey, Adam! Genius! Can you help me with math? Please?"

"No problem!" Adam cheerfully pulled a chair over to face Callum's desk. I watched to see if Callum would just end up copying Adam's homework, but that didn't happen. Adam explained the rule and patiently talked Callum through the steps on the hopelessly outdated scientific calculator that the school had provided.

"Adam, thank you *so* much—that was mad helpful," Callum said when the bell rang.

"Yeah . . . Adam, you're a good teacher," I told Adam, who was packing up his planner. "I really appreciate your helping out."

Adam smiled. "It's all my math teacher, Ms. Lambert," he said. "She explains everything very clearly—it's impossible *not* to be interested!"

I stared at him, open-mouthed.

"I'll see you later, Miss Garon," he said, gathering the remainder of his stuff and strolling off to his next class.

———

Teachers had to send out midterm reports to any students running a 65 or lower in their respective classes.

"Adam, you didn't get any reports, did you?" I asked, not looking up from the ones I was filling out. We were in study hall again. I noticed Adam's desk had somehow made its way over to abut mine. Callum's was in satellite orbit nearby.

He paused a little too long before answering. I looked up. He cringed.

"Nooo!" I cried. "What subject could you possibly be failing?"

"It's gym," he said mournfully.

"*Gym?* What the hell, Adam? All you have to do to pass gym is participate. Oh, and wear deodorant. And change into stupid clothes."

"That's the problem."

"Huh?"

"I haven't been wearing the right sneakers," he said vaguely.

I looked down at his feet. He was wearing black penny loafers.

"Why not? What do they require?"

"White soles."

"So, wear the right ones. What's the problem?"

He squirmed uncomfortably, and I realized with horror that I had made a crucial miscalculation. I had unconsciously taken Adam's slacks and button-downs to be a sign of, if not wealth, at least relative comfort compared to other kids in the school. I understood suddenly that he wasn't wearing his church clothes to make a fashion statement. These were his *only* clothes—at least, the only presentable ones. No wonder he seemed to have so many blue shirts. He must have washed and ironed the same two or three several times a week.

Adam was looking at me. "Hey, it's okay," he said, with an attempt at levity. "I'll get 'em soon . . . no biggie."

I have to make this right, I thought. I wouldn't be able to look Adam in the eye otherwise. So I stood up next to him, and playfully lined up my own small, pink-sneakered foot next to his. "Hey, well, I'd lend you mine, but I'm not sure we're the same size. . . ."

He grinned. "Yours have spikes anyway," he said. Since my first year, I had taken to wearing Puma track shoes to school for reasons too idiosyncratic to explain. "They're against the rules—they'd wreck the gym floor."

"Rules, rules. What shoe size are these canal boats anyway, big guy? Twenty-five?"

"Right. Twenty-five," he said, rolling his eyes. "Try eleven?"

A period later, I left the building under the pretense of going to buy lunch. Instead, I headed for the discount shoe store near the 2 train.

"I need men's shoes, size eleven, with white soles," I told the salesman.

He picked up a box from the display case and opened them for me. "These look okay?"

I peered in. They were Champions, a brand I recognized from my own youth. It wasn't Nike, but it wouldn't fall apart right away either.

"How much?"

"For you, $30."

As I reentered the building, a nosy, twenty-year veteran teacher from the main school looked at me suspiciously.

"What's in the bag?" she growled, in her six-pack-a-day smoker voice. "You know you're not supposed to be using prep periods for your personal errands."

I had always been scared of this woman. The fact that she no longer governed me made no difference. "I'm on lunch," I said. "And I had to get something for a student."

"You got shoes for a student?" She glared at the logo on the bag and growled, "You can't do that! If you do that for one kid, they'll all start wanting them! Never do that again! Go demand that your principal give you back your money!"

I fought back tears. I needed to do this; it was penitence.

"I'll deal with it." I ran upstairs before she could see how she had upset me.

I realized I did not know how to give Adam the shoes. I did not want him to know they were from me—at least, not with any certainty. And I couldn't let on to any of the other kids.

In the end, I decided to chance another administrator. I went to the school secretary.

"Can you give these to Adam?" I asked her.

"Awww, you bought him shoes? Honey, that's so sweet!"

"Listen—don't tell him they're from me. Say . . . say they're from the 'Committee for the Importance of Gym' or something. Or say they're from the PTA. Whatever."

"We don't have a PTA."

"Whatever—say anything! Just don't tell him they're from me!"

I made it to ninth period before my little secret was found out. As I was getting ready to leave, Adam appeared in my classroom, bag of shoes in hands. His face was tear-streaked, but he was beaming.

"Miss, someone got me sneakers!" he said.

"Great—now you have no excuse for not passing gym." I busied myself wiping the board, despite the fact that it was blank.

"See, the funny thing is, the secretary says they're from the PTA. . . ."

"Well, isn't that nice."

"But I know we don't have a PTA."

"Hmm. Interesting."

"So . . . you know who I think they're from?"

"Beats me. I've never seen these shoes in my life."

"Oh, Miss Garon," he said, his eyes welling up again. "You are ridiculous!" He grabbed me with both arms, and hugged me to his chest so tightly that I nearly choked.

———

If I had had a "teaching husband," a partner in raising my adorable brood of 115 high school students, it would have been Dan.

He was a science teacher, about a year and a half younger than I was. It was his first year teaching, and my first year in the small school, so we got along brilliantly. We taught all the same kids. He was creative, brilliant, and totally scattered. He was also gay: "Cute barrettes," he had told me one day early in the year, by way of a greeting. "My boyfriend, some of the other teachers, and I are going drinking tonight. Wanna come?"

I loved Dan. I loved his earnest brown eyes, the way he would crack up laughing whenever we were really stressed out (leading me to do the same), and his passion for making science exciting to the kids. I was envious of his zany lesson plans. One time, he had the kids create a double helix DNA strand out of multicolored lollypops. If they did it right, they were allowed to eat the lollypops afterwards. The kids loved it, and I wished I had thought of it, despite the fact that I wasn't even teaching science.

"I don't want the kids to know I'm gay," he had told me early on.

"Why?"

"Because I don't know if they'll respect me."

We were sitting in the science lab after school, grading papers.

"You know, I think you could do a lot of good if you came out," I told him, instantly thinking of Adam, who was so tough and capable, and yet probably needed a mentor badly—one who could identify with him better than I could. "Like, there might be so many gay and questioning kids here who are afraid to come out and who really need a role model. You could form a Gay-Straight Alliance. Hell, I'd cochair it with you."

He looked at me with a cocked eyebrow. "Easy for you to say—you'd be the straight half of the alliance."

I shut up.

Some of the kids wondered. Periodically, I would hear them speculating about him in class. But most of them not only thought that he was straight—they thought that we were dating. At one point, he and I were walking to the train station together when a group of kids ran out of a neighborhood pizza joint, screaming with delight and throwing their books in the air. "We knew it! We knew you were going out!" they cried, deliriously happy. Apparently, our walk to the subway together had been just the confirmation they needed. Dan and I just looked at each other and laughed. After that, whenever I was looking for Dan, I would say, "Hey, do you guys know where my *boyfriend* is?" and they'd all fall about in stitches.

Most of them were fooled. Except for Adam.

Dan came to me midsemester and handed me a tiny folded piece of paper. "What the hell do I do about this?" He looked anxious.

I opened the paper and instantly recognized Adam's handwriting, though I didn't tell Dan. *Dear Mr. C.,* it read. *I think you are the most handsome teacher ever, and brilliant as well. I'm in love with you. I know you are the youngest teacher in the school, and I wonder if you would consider dating someone only a few years younger than yourself . . .* It went on like this for about a page, and then was signed, *Your Secret Admirer.*

"It's from me," I said, looking up and refolding the piece of paper. "I'm your secret admirer. Take me to bed or lose me forever."

He rolled his eyes. "You and I both know it's from Adam."

"You . . . I mean, we do?"

"Yes! He's only been mooning around my classroom every single day this week."

"Crap." I had known Adam was lonely from day one, when he had said on his index card that he wished he had a new boyfriend. But this seemed rash for a kid who was normally so self-possessed and mature. That he would make such drastic overtures to catch the attention of the one other semi-openly gay man in the school made me realize one thing: Adam was desperate.

"What do you want to do about this?" I asked Dan.

"I don't know. I just don't want this to be, you know, where everyone finds out. . . ." He looked at me meaningfully.

"He and I are close," I said. "Can I talk to him for you?"

———

I pulled Adam aside at lunch. "You got a few minutes?" I asked him.

"Of course!" He looked so thrilled to see me that I felt awful for the blow I was about to deliver.

I led him into an empty classroom and we each sat in a desk and faced each other. For a couple of minutes we made small talk. Then I got to the point.

"Okay. We have to discuss something," I said.

He looked concerned. "What is it?"

"The letter you sent to Dan—I mean, uh, to Mr. C."

"I didn't send him a letter," he said, looking down at the desk.

"Adam, come on. I know it was you. I know your handwriting."

"He showed it to you? I mean—what's wrong with my sending him a complimentary letter?" He was on the defensive now; I could hear it in the rising pitch of his voice.

I sighed. "Adam, you just can't send letters like that to teachers. It's completely inappropriate."

"But—"

"Shh. Listen," I said, putting my hand up. "You know as well as I do that students and teachers can't have romantic relationships. It's incredibly illegal. You can't ask out your teacher, the same way they can't ask you out. If anything like that is even *suspected*, a teacher can lose his or her job. Look. I know you really like Dan. He's a great guy. But do you understand what an awkward and vulnerable position you're putting him in, especially with his being a new teacher?"

By now Adam was crying. He made no effort to hide the tears streaming down his face.

"It's just so lonely," he sobbed. "You don't know how it is being the only one."

I took his hand and held it. We sat quietly for a few moments until his sobbing quieted. I did not know what to say; I felt terrible.

"Hey," I finally said. "You okay?" He sniffed in response. "Sweetheart, listen. High school is just . . . I don't know . . . rotten. Seriously. Anyone who ever tells you high school was the best time of their life is either a complete idiot or a liar."

He grinned half-heartedly.

"I know you've got it tough." I watched tears spring back into his eyes. "Being gay here must be . . . maddening."

He wiped his eyes.

"I guess college . . . well, I think you'll have a million boyfriends. High school . . ." I paused, thinking for an accurate metaphor. "Well, my mom says high school is like being tricked into going on a first date dressed in a chicken suit. I feel like that pretty much sums it up."

At this, he laughed a little bit. I felt relieved, though I knew it was only because he was allowing me to.

"It sucks," I said. "But you'll get through it."

"I know I will," he said.

Date:	October 1, 2005
To:	Family, friends, and enemies
Subject:	Stupid fights, as opposed to the really well thought-out ones . . .
From:		Signature:	

The kids are somewhat better behaved in this school; it makes me wonder what the teachers they drove out would have done if they'd ever taught at Explorers. Due to the fact that the kids' parents have to sign them up for the program, the school is ensured a student body whose families place some emphasis on education; this was certainly not the case in the school I came from (downstairs). Academically, they're not much more advanced, but they are significantly more focused. There are far fewer problems with truancy, and when I assign homework most of them actually do it.

They also get excited about learning. Last week I prepared some scenes for them to act out. By my third English class of the day, word had gotten around that we were doing skits in class, and so the kids came in saying "Are we acting? Can I have a part?" I was surprised and pleased by their enthusiasm.

One thing that has stayed the same is the consistent fighting. Besides the gang problems that are endemic to the building (no more to one school small or big school within it than another), the kids are really unable to resolve any dispute without a full-on war.

It's funny, actually, because their fights are so unbelievably stupid: In Explorers, kids would fight over whose sneakers were cooler or if you took a dig at someone's mother. Here, they fight over being interrupted in class. On Wednesday, I called on a girl named Michaela, listened to her speak, and then said, "Good job, Michaela. Shadae, would you like to add anything?" Michaela said, "I'm not finished." Shadae retorted, "Oh yes you are." They immediately started screaming obscenities and pounding each other into the ground. Two of the big boys and I pried them apart, while a third ran to get security. It was dramatic.

The following day, another altercation: A girl named Kara asked the teacher a question about the dress code, which another girl, Janelle, took to be a dig at her, implying that she was (*gasp!*) not following the dress code. This fight spilled out into the hallway with screams of "Who you callin' a skank???" and the ensuing beat down that was thankfully broken up by security quickly.

So it's definitely not perfect. But it is a significant improvement, and I feel very hopeful that this year will be better than the last two. I am enjoying being able to teach more academically and doing less behavior modification; already, we've done a small unit on prejudice and hate crime legislation, written several short essays, and gotten through a good chunk of *To Kill a Mockingbird* without allegations of racism on either my part or Harper Lee's, so this seems like progress.

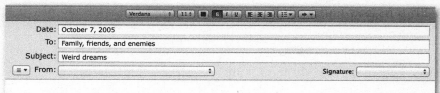

Even after now that I've been in my "new" small school a couple of
months, which is decidedly less "crazy" than Explorers, I still keep having
this particular recurring dream. It's one I've had consistently over the past
couple of years. In it, I'm sitting in class, and all of a sudden one of the
students raises a gun out of nowhere and points it at the back of another
kid's head. Then I wake up, sweating.

Verdana · 11 · ■ B *I* U 三 三 三 三▼ ➔▼

Date: November 18, 2005
To: Family, friends, and enemies
Subject: Oddly enough, teaching is easier when you can talk . . .
From: [   ] Signature: [   ]

Things are very busy, but generally good. This week was difficult because I lost my voice. Not being able to yell would have been murder in Explorers proper (or "Big Explorers," as we call it), but the kids here at least pretend to do what you tell them to. I put up instructions for group work on the board, and then delegated a student to make announcements for me. This involved me whispering in dulcet tones to said student, who would then scream whatever I'd said across the classroom, along with whatever other announcements s/he felt like making ("And by the way, Christina and Carl are going out"). So things worked out okay, well, at least with the eleventh-graders. . . .

My ninth-grade math kids were another story and basically act like the kids in Big Explorers, except that they're actually the age they're supposed to be because they haven't been held back several times. With them, it's constantly "Ms. Garon! He's touching me!" and "No, he touched me *first!*" and "She stole my pen!" and "Shanice is looking at me!"

I separate them, reseat them, call homes, etc. When I come into the room every day, I basically have to "unclump" them, since they're always on top of each other play-fighting in varying degrees. It's fabulous. Periodically I have the urge to say, "Oh, act your age!" and then I remember they're fourteen and think saying "Don't act your age!" would probably be a more appropriate course of action. . . .

Many of them, in some clingy display of ninth-grade love that I don't quite understand, like to bring their chairs right up to my desk and work around me. Usually this just causes me to trip on their chairs every time I move, but in this case it was useful, because I could whisper to them while they did their work, and the few remaining kids who didn't feel the need to be right up in my armpits all the time were generally able to avoid killing each other.

I do have to say that teaching math has been (and continues to be) interesting. I'm consistently surprised both by how much I remember from my own high school years and by how much I've forgotten. So far I've taught concepts like frequency, cumulative frequency, and probability, as well as reviewed things like exponents, signed numbers (negative or positive), and order of operations. My best ideas have involved giving everyone colored pens to fill in their histograms to show the different frequencies, and using bags with different kinds of candy to demonstrate probability: "So if there are seven Jolly Ranchers and six Snickers, and Tyler picks a Snickers on his turn, then if Blessing picks randomly what is the probability he will draw a Snickers as well?"

Trying to figure out how to teach math has been interesting for me. Mostly I follow the lessons that are provided for me by a senior math teacher, but I have to review the information myself the night before to make sure I know it, and trying to explain verbally always requires some thought, especially since I was never that great at math to begin with. But overall, it's been a pretty interesting challenge, and I don't regret having taken it on—not that I had any choice in the matter.

CHAPTER TEN

Alfredo

Alfredo came to my tenth-grade English class with a reputation. This, in itself, was not noteworthy; there were other kids known for starting problems, and I didn't even know what Alfredo looked like until the moment he walked into my classroom the first day. Other teachers, however, were constantly telling me stories about fights he had started, terrible things he had said and done in class. The previous year, he had actually been suspended for hitting a teacher, who had subsequently told me that he had threatened to wait for her out by her car and "jump her" after school. For this, he had received a sixty-day suspension. I had seen teachers in the lounge, reduced to tears, who had only replied "Alfredo" when I had asked what was wrong.

"Watch out for that kid; he's nuts," the veteran teachers told me.

Even Alfredo's older sister, Elyssa, who I am fairly certain had stolen my wallet the previous semester (though she never admitted it), stopped me in the stairwell to ask if he was behaving.

"Yeah, he's fine," I told her. There was nothing about his appearance to suggest menace—he was a skinny boy of about five feet, six inches with brown hair in a short buzz cut and tanned skin. He wore a hearing aid in one ear. In the couple of weeks since school had begun, all Alfredo had done was come up to my desk and touch things on it without permission. "Hey, silly guy, go sit down now," I had told him mildly, wanting to defuse any potential conflict. He had grinned and done just what I had asked.

His sister laughed at my naïveté. "Wait," she said.

I was perplexed. The only thing remotely problematic about Alfredo, as far as I could tell, was that every quiz he turned in was either blank or totally unintelligible. That, and his attendance. But there were other students like that.

Then, a month or so into the term, I got my first glimpse of what made Alfredo so infamous. We were studying Shakespeare's *Julius Caesar*. The students were in groups, clipping magazine pictures to make MySpace or Facebook pages for the characters in the play. On a profile for Caesar himself, for instance, the students listed "tyranny, killing Pompeii, becoming king," and of course, "my hot wife Calpurnia" in the Interests category. There was giggling all over the room.

Alfredo was not participating. I came up to him and said, "Alfredo, don't you want to join a group?"

He looked up at me with irritation and said, in his best imitation of a gangster voice, "I'm not doing this shit. Do you know who I am? Do you *know* who I *am*?"

I looked up at the students, who were now staring in our direction. In a moment of inspiration, I called out in a mock announcer's voice, "Ladies and gentleman, this poor boy is having a problem: He cannot remember his name. Can anyone identify him?"

There was a moment of dead silence, and then the kids burst out laughing. "Ooooh, snap!" they yelled. Alfredo sunk into his seat and ignored us all for the rest of the period.

The following week, the students were taking turns reading the parts out loud. I could never get them to act—despite their willingness to make fools of themselves yelling out goofy comments in class ("Brutus is a G!"), they would all suddenly develop stage fright when pressed to perform in front of their classmates. Reading aloud was the most I could get from them.

I was sitting on the desk following along with their reading when I happened to look over at Alfredo and saw that he was not even looking at his copy of the play. Instead, he was feverishly writing in his notebook.

"Alfredo, open up the play and follow along with the reading, okay?" I said to him. I walked over to his desk and looked at what he was doing.

"I'm just taking notes, Miss," he said, pulling his notebook towards him. But he was not quick enough; I saw "Dear Stephanie" on the top of the page before he hid it from me. I had to chuckle. Stephanie was his girlfriend who, in one of her rare guest appearances in school, happened to be sitting right next to him.

"Please put that away," I told him. "You can do it later."

"Okay," he said and motioned to put his notebook back into his bag.

I continued on with the class, but noticed that several of the students were now looking in Alfredo's direction. I followed their gazes. He was writing the love letter to Stephanie again, while she appeared to be looking over at the paper with amusement.

"Alfredo, what did I just tell you? You're going to miss the important part—Julius Caesar's about to get murdered!"

The kids started protesting. "Miss! You know if it was me you'd have taken that note away a long time ago," one of them shouted out. He was right, of course. But I had not forgotten everything I had been told about Alfredo. I did not want to provoke him.

"Okay. Alfredo, put the note away or I'm going to take it," I said.

Alfredo looked up at me and smirked. Again, he motioned to put the book back in his bag. He looked up right before putting it in to make sure my sight was still trained on him.

"Alfredo, put it in your backpack," I said, sternly. Then, when I made sure he'd put it away, I said, "Great. Starting where we left off . . . who's reading Brutus's part again?"

We finished the reading, and I told the kids to get into trios for group work. I looked over at Alfredo, who was making no effort to join a group. He was working on his letter to Stephanie again. Presently, he ripped it out of his notebook, folded it, and reached over to pass it to Stephanie.

I got there first.

"*Yoink!*" I said, and plucked the folded paper from his outstretched hand. He was too surprised to stop me. Stephanie, who had not been paying attention, looked surprised, as well.

"Give that back!" he yelled.

"Alfredo, you know the rules. And I asked you multiple times to put it away," I told him. "Now, if you do your group work like you're supposed to, I'll give it back to you at the end of the period." Then I stuck the note in my pocket and went off to help the other students.

Alfredo did not join a group. Instead, he sat there sulking until the end of the period. "Stupid white bitch," I heard him mutter to his girlfriend, who wasn't doing group work either.

When the bell rang at the end of the period, he approached me.

"Yo, give me my note back now."

"Alfredo, I told you that you'd get it back if you participated. But you didn't. You sat in the back of the room talking trash," I told him firmly. "You didn't keep your part of the bargain, so you may not have your note back. I won't read it, but I am throwing it out."

"What?" he replied, instantly enraged again. "I spent all period on that note!"

"Right. And you should have been following along with the reading."

"What the f—! Stupid white bitch, f—ing me over! I'mma f— you up, you hear me?" He stepped up close to me, shuffling on his feet in some sort of wrestling stance and yelling in my face. "White bitches is always f—ing me over!" Then he reached toward me.

I was caught off guard by his fury and stood frozen in place. One kid, Michael, suddenly stepped between Alfredo and me. Michael was a tall kid with a perpetually angry look on his face who would snarl at me whenever I tried to show him the place in the reading.

But now, Michael's behavior could only have been described as quasi-religious. "Alfredo, my man," he said, in a voice so calm it would have persuaded a gunman to release hostages, "Chill, my man. Be cool."

I stepped around Michael, who had now placed his hands paternally on Alfredo's shoulders. Alfredo was staring up at him, awed. I ran out of the room just as Alfredo came to and resumed his tirade, following me out into the hall: "F—ing white bitch! She stole my note! I'mma f— her up, that bitch!" This time security heard him, and the principal, Mr. Carver, came out of his office.

"What happened?" he asked me.

"Alfredo freaked out because I took away a note he was writing to Stephanie," I told Carver. I stuck the folded letter into Carver's shirt pocket. Then I ran off to class.

Because Alfredo had both threatened me ("I'mma f— you up!") and employed a racist epithet ("Damn white bitches!"), the charges were doubled. The school decided to seek a superintendent's suspension of sixty days, like the one Alfredo had received for his previous teacher-threatening escapade.

To do this, there had to be a Board of Education hearing, which, in what the principal told me was a clear effort to get the charges dropped out of sheer inconvenience, was called for the day of parent-teacher conferences. The hearing ran like a miniature trial. There were witnesses, evidence presented, a lawyer for the defendant (although I am told that was unusual), and a judge, who was an old retired superintendent with a huge white handlebar mustache. The courtroom resembled a conference room with everyone seated around a large elliptical table – the judge, our principal, our dean of security, another teacher who had witnessed Alfredo's behavior, Alfredo's mother, Alfredo's lawyer, Alfredo's lawyer's assistant, Alfredo's witness, Alfredo, and me.

The witness was Alfredo's now ex-girlfriend, Stephanie. The day before the trial, Alfredo had apparently called her a "stupid ho" and told her that he did not respect her. For this, she had slapped him in the face and said, "We're through." Yet, she was still here, dutifully supporting him. She would not meet my eyes.

At the beginning of the hearing, we went around the table and everyone introduced him or herself. When it got to my turn, Alfredo's lawyer immediately piped in, "Your honor, could you please ask Ms. Garon to speak up? My client is deaf in one ear!"

Alfredo's hearing was just fine with the hearing aid, and everyone knew it. Also, I was sitting directly across the table from him. It was a clear play on the judge's sympathies, calculated to fluster me.

I said my name very clearly again and looked at the judge. Out of the corner of my eye, I saw Alfredo smirk.

The lawyer had, I believe, learned everything he knew about the legal system from watching *Law & Order* reruns. He came prepared with a lengthy opening statement, the gist of which was that our school had fabricated the entire charge because we had a longstanding vendetta against Alfredo. When the lawyer finished his speech, he looked pleased with himself. Then he turned towards me.

"Ms. Garon. You look very young; how long have you been teaching?"

"I'm twenty-five, and this is my third year," I told him.

"Where were you on the date in question?"

"In Alfredo's class. Fifth period."

"And what happened in that class?"

I proceeded to recount the entire incident, from my first effort to get Alfredo to put the note away, to Alfredo's threat.

"And what happened after that?" the lawyer asked. I wondered where this was going.

"After that, I left the classroom, passed Mr. Carver—our principal—in the hallway, gave him the note, and went to my next class, sixth-period English," I responded.

"And what was the lesson plan that day?"

I wanted to say, "Is this really relevant?" but instead I looked at the judge, who had clearly thought the same thing, because he flared his mustache and said to the lawyer, "Please stick to the point, counselor!"

"Ms. Garon," said the lawyer. He had that same smug expression that he'd had when asking me to repeat my name. "You stated that Alfredo was writing and passing notes in class. Is that correct?"

"Yes."

"But you stated that you confiscated his note to Stephanie, right?"

"Yes, I did."

He looked incredibly pleased with himself now. I figured he must be coming to his point. "In that case," he said, pausing dramatically and cocking an eyebrow, "could you *really* say he was 'passing' notes if you intercepted his note *before* he passed it?"

Alfredo's mother was sitting in the corner, having been moved from the round table for my cross-examination. She was at least six feet tall, extremely obese, and was scribbling furiously on a three-inch notepad. Now, she looked up at me and said "Mmmmhmmm!" as loudly as she could.

I turned to the judge for help. He didn't say anything, so I said, "Your honor—the point isn't the semantics of whether or not he was 'passing' notes! He was off-task, the other students were distracted, he ignored instructions, and then he threatened me!"

Alfredo's lawyer now looked irritated at me. The judge remained impassive. He said, "That's all for now," and sent me out of the room, into the hallway, with instructions to send the principal in after me.

I waited in the hallway for a good couple of hours, being summoned back into the room sporadically for a few seconds at a time to clarify things like whether I had spoken to the principal after fifth period or after sixth period.

While I was waiting, the dean of security showed me some of the statements the students had made, which were being submitted for evidence. Half the students had apparently failed to notice the entire altercation or forgotten it the moment the bell rang. The other half had prepared statements that made me, as their English teacher, hang my head in shame: *Alfredo be beastin' on Ms. Garon, called her a white bitch. Why he be beastin'? I do not know.*

One statement stuck out from the rest. It was Stephanie's. It said: *Alfredo was doing his work like he was supposed to. Then Ms. Garon yelled at him for no reason. He didn't do nothing.*

Her statement made my stomach tighten because I feared it might be true. I asked myself why I had felt the need to confiscate his note in the first place, why I had not left well-enough alone. He had not been harming anyone. Why hadn't I just let him write the damn note?

Of course, I knew the answer: Because the class had been watching. My hold on them was so tenuous already. I could not afford to lose face in front of the other twenty-nine students. And now, because of whom that thirtieth student was—a kid with an out-of-control temper who belonged in some specialized program—we were all here in Board of Ed court, missing parent-teacher conferences.

Around 2 p.m., about five hours after we had started, the trial let out. We drove back to the school as fast as we could, in an effort to catch the last fifteen minutes of conferences. We would not find out the ruling until that weekend, but Mr. Carver was confident—he told us, chuckling, that in trying to prove how often Alfredo was unjustly barred from attending school, the lawyer had accidentally revealed the reason Alfredo had been suspended the year before.

"That lawyer—what an idiot," he said, looking tired but pleased.

The ruling was, as Mr. Carver predicted, in our favor. Alfredo would be gone for another sixty days.

After the trial, I went to talk to the parent coordinator, a handsome middle-aged woman who had kids in one of the other small schools in the building. She was savvy and tended to be a helpful source of information that might not otherwise be in the kids' files—at least, not the parts I had access to.

"What's the deal with Alfredo, anyway?" I asked her. "Why is his mom so intent on keeping him in this school, even while he's on his second sixty-day suspension?"

She closed the door to her office before speaking to me. "You can't repeat what I'm about to tell you," she said. "Do you know what a Nickerson letter is?"

"No."

"It's a letter from the school board, saying that they can't provide the right services for your kid, so they'll pay for you to send him somewhere else, like a private school." She paused, and then added wistfully, "God, I would kill for one of those for my kids, you know?"

"Yeah . . ."

"So, Alfredo's mom has a Nickerson letter. They offered it to her after he hit and threatened that special ed teacher last year. She can send Alfredo anywhere she wants. That's how badly they want him out."

"Why is he still here then?"

"She won't take him out. She says it's because she wants to keep him near Elyssa," the parent coordinator told me, rolling her eyes at the implausibility of this excuse. "But seriously, I've spoken to her about this." She paused and then said conspiratorially, "I think she is literally waiting for something bad to happen with him involved, and then she's going to try to sue the school for a million dollars."

After he left, the students seemed to forget about Alfredo. Supposedly, he was attending a program for suspended students. His teachers were supposed to fax him homework once a week, which we did. Then his mother was supposed to return it to us to be graded, so as to avoid Alfredo losing any credit.

In fact, Alfredo got kicked out of the suspended students' center for allegedly inciting a riot within a week of being there. This is what I heard, anyway. After that, he stayed home all day. The guidance counselor said she had called him to find out if he was actually doing his homework. According to her, he sounded stoned.

Several months later, the dean of security came into the teacher's lounge when a bunch of us were sitting around grading papers.

"I have an announcement," he said. We put our paper stacks down and listened. "Alfredo will be coming back next week, and . . . I just want to warn you all that, historically, we've had some problems—"

He didn't finish because we all started booing. "Aww, man! Whose class is he going to be in now?" someone asked.

"Actually, we're putting him into a ninth-grade special education track, with Liz," said the dean. "He needs to make up the credits anyway, and the 'plan' is that we'll be better able to control him in a self-contained environment."

What the dean neglected to acknowledge was that Liz, the special education teacher in question, was in her first year. Was putting him in the hands of the *least* experienced faculty member possibly part of the "plan" as well?

Liz was understandably nervous. "Do you think he'll be awful still?" she asked me. "I have to be in the room alone with him. . . ." She looked upset. I promised her that I would go hang out in her class and grade papers during my free period so she wouldn't be alone with him, questioning all the while whether this would serve as a helpful influence or just the opposite.

As it turned out, neither Liz nor I should have worried. Alfredo didn't show up for class at all during his first two weeks back, preferring instead to loiter outside the school and in the hallways between classes. I saw him making out with several different girls, not one of whom was Stephanie, who seemed to be ignoring him with an almost fierce pride. Then, in his second week back, he got angry at a school police officer who had stopped him at scanning. One thing led to another and he ended up punching the cop. When he was flat on the ground with his wrists cuffed, a moment later, Alfredo reportedly said to one of the cops, who was chummy with the kids, "Officer Diaz—can you come here a minute?"

"No Alfredo, you can speak to me from here," said Officer Diaz.

"No, seriously. Officer Diaz, can you come here?" he said again, jerking his head sideways in a "come hither" gesture.

"Alfredo—what are you talking about?" The cops searched him and found an eighth of pot on him.

I wondered, after the fact, why Alfredo thought Officer Diaz could get him out of that one.

But apparently, all this only served to make Alfredo more attractive to the several different girls he was dating. Sometime after Alfredo was taken away in cuffs, this time not to return to school, a sign appeared in black magic marker on the wall of the girls' bathroom, reading:

Kara – Step off my man bitch! – Jazmyn

Shortly thereafter, a reply showed up on the same wall:

Jazmyn – Meet me in the hallway 7th period. Bitch! – Kara

Seventh period came, and the hair extensions were flying. The hall was crowded with screaming kids. In the center, five different girls, two of whom were the aforementioned Kara and Jazmyn, were piled on top of each other. Rather than the boys, who would throw punches, the girls would hold each other in death grips, trying to slam each other into floors or walls and pull each other's hair out. Their faces were greased with Vaseline, to prevent their eyes from being clawed by the inch-long painted fingernails of their rivals, and their respective handmaidens stood at the sides, holding their jewelry and sweatshirts patiently.

The beleaguered cops pushed the crowds aside and separated the girls, cuffing them even as they still continued to swing at each other. As the girls were hauled off, cuffed, in different directions, one of them began leaping around screaming, "I love you Alfredo! I'mma fight for you! I'mma die for you, Alfredo!" The others joined, seemingly oblivious not only to the fact that Alfredo had clearly been unfaithful to all of them, but also to the fact that he was not present.

I was standing in the doorway to my room with several of the boys from my class. As we stared at the floor of the hallway, now littered with straight braids, one of the boys turned to me, a look of awe on his face. He seemed to be searching for words.

"Something on your mind, mister?" I asked.

"Miss Garon," he said in a reverential tone, "girls is crazy!"

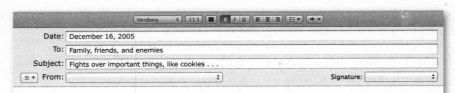

Date: December 16, 2005
To: Family, friends, and enemies
Subject: Fights over important things, like cookies . . .
From: Signature:

The week started out with this punk freshman interrupting me midsentence during a lesson on the distributive property to ask, "Yo miss. You not a virgin, right?" I said, without raising my voice, "That's totally inappropriate, I'm calling your parents," which I did, and then after saying "Oh no he didn't!" a few times, they cancelled Christmas on him. Haha. He then wrote me a letter of apology explaining that he didn't know what a virgin was. I have trouble buying that, being that he's fourteen.

Meanwhile, one of the other freshman, a little girl who daydreams constantly during math and always whips out her anime novels the minute I start writing on the board, said matter-of-factly, "Miss, you can't call my home, because whenever you call my home I get whipped." I said, "What?" She showed me her arm. Up and down it there were red welts and huge bruises. I said, "Are you serious?" She said, "Yeah, they always hit me with belts." Poor kid was getting the you-know-what beaten out of her. I filed a report with the guidance counselors, who immediately called ACS. I was assuming she'd be terribly angry with me . . . most kids are after I do the mandated reporter shtick. But apparently she was incredibly cooperative with the guidance counselors, and when I had her for math the next day she acted like nothing had happened whatsoever.

That same afternoon, a fight broke out in front of my classroom. Stephanie had apparently been "looking" at Jazmine's boyfriend. So Stephanie and Jazmine went at it, with hundreds of kids (where do they *come* from???) stamping and hollering in the audience. Presently, Kiara ran up in there and said to Jazmine, "What? You was too pussy to fight me, and now you fightin' her?" and promptly joined the fight, offended over having been slighted in her opportunity for violence earlier. How stupid is that? The football players and I separated the girls, and then the cops come and handcuffed everyone, including some girl who isn't even involved, but just wanted to retrieve her jacket from the general melee.

A second fight broke out a couple of periods later: In an eleventh-grade math class for which I was subbing, Calvin had brought in some cookies, which got eaten. So Calvin tried to hold the entire class hostage at the end of the period saying, "No one leaves this room until I get my cookies back!" And this other girl, Josie, who happened to have her hair dyed bright red and braided into cornrows, said (rightfully), "Shut up you idiot! We're trying to work!" And Calvin responded brilliantly, "Yeah? Go get some real hair!" Now them's fightin' words (just like derisive remarks about sneakers, coats, or mamas), so the two of them went at it, aided by various acolytes, until the school safety cops broke it up and everyone went to peer-mediation.

But truthfully, I was rooting for the girl with dreads on that one. . . . The guy with the cookie issue (by the way, his cookies were quietly eaten by a third student who wasn't even involved in the fight) is chronically truant, a slacker, a jerk, an idiot, has a mother who always makes excuses for him, and is generally a royal pain in my ass. Plus the girl with dreads is half his size, and I always root for the underdog.

CHAPTER ELEVEN

Destiny & Anthony

Destiny—despite her name—was small and quiet. She was in the tenth-grade class that I taught first period, which by all accounts was too early: kids were constantly coming in late, still buckling the belts they'd had to remove at scanning. Looking around the classroom, they would appear bewildered as to how they had gotten there and what they were supposed to be doing—"C'mon Miss, why you always asking me if I have a pen? You think I work at Staples or something?" Once settled in their desks, they would cradle their chins in their palms and stare off into space, only coming to when I called on them. One of the girls, Jessica, would even come in with a piece of blue cloth on which she had sprinkled Davidoff's Cool Water fragrance. She would sit at her desk sucking her thumb, holding the cloth up to her nose so that she could continually inhale the scent.

"Smell it, Miss. It's mad nice," she offered politely when I asked her if it was really necessary to bring a security blanket to tenth-grade English.

To be completely honest, I loved first period. As I did not feel much more energetic than they did at 8 a.m., I privately thanked God for their complacency. I would generally start the period by teaching a brief lesson—writing on the board, calling on a couple of students, Socratic style—and then break them into pairs for group work. The kids, happy not to have anything too challenging demanded of them, would work cooperatively until the bell rang. Though half their class could never be bothered to show up, the best grades I gave were inevitably to the first-period kids; since they didn't have the energy to goof off, like the later classes, they actually paid attention.

Destiny was one of the lone exceptions to this rule. She was in class most days, but instead of just looking sleepy or mystified by her surroundings like the rest of her peers, she just seemed miserable. Her head would be down on the desk from the moment I entered the room until the bell rang; then, she would wearily gather her books and leave. More often than not, I would see tears running down her cheeks.

In the first few days of class, I tried by the usual means to find out what was going on. "Destiny, is everything okay?" I asked her, squatting beside her desk. The girls within earshot looked towards us with glances of sympathy and confusion; the boys did not appear to be paying any attention.

Destiny nodded.

"Okay, that's good . . . is there anything you want to talk to me about?"

She shook her head.

"Girl, level with me: Are you in 'that time of the month'? Do you need to go to the nurse?" Cramps were often the culprit when I found girls with their heads down, although I suspected that if the answer were so simple, I would already have heard about it. They tended not to be shy about that sort of thing.

Destiny shook her head again emphatically and then put it back down on her desk.

After repeating this nonconversation several days in a row, I gave up and called her home. Destiny's mother answered.

"Who is this?" The question was flat, bored.

"Hi, this is Ms. Garon, Destiny's English teacher . . . she might have mentioned the essay for my class . . . no? Anyway, I'm concerned . . . she always seems very tired in my class, like she hasn't slept. I know it's first period, but she never takes her head off the desk. And she just seems sad. . . ."

The mother didn't respond.

"Ms. . . . Rodriguez?"

"It's her boyfriend, Anthony," her mother finally said. She seemed to think this needed no further explanation. I could hear the TV on in the background.

"Um . . . what about Anthony? Have they just broken up?"

"No, they talk on the phone all night."

"Oh. Well, could you tell her to go to bed earlier?"

"Yeah, Okay, I'll tell her." Same bored tone. Then, with a click, and she hung up.

I went to see the social worker, Alice. Her office was comfortable— well air-conditioned, with a rug and colorful beanbag chairs. My first instinct was to be jealous of her accommodations until it dawned on me that she had brought in all these amenities herself in an effort to make the office inviting for the kids.

"This is a great office," I told her.

Alice smiled. "Thanks! I wish we could get rid of the mice though. . . ."

"Mice?" I jumped in alarm. I noticed there were traps in the corners. "Ugh! I'm so sorry you have to deal with that—I'm terrified of those suckers," I admitted.

"Yeah, so gross! I hear them skittering around sometimes when I'm here alone late in the afternoon." She shivered. "So what's going on?"

"Well, I'm not sure what you can tell me about this," I said. "But I have this student . . . Destiny. . . ."

Alice sighed.

"So you've met her," I said.

"Yes."

"What's her deal? Why is she always sad?"

She appeared to think for a second. "Well, she has lots of problems . . . but mostly it's her boyfriend. Do you know Anthony Hall?"

The last name cued my memory. I vaguely knew the face that belonged with it, though I had never taught him—he was a tall, bulky football player with dark skin and a close-cropped Caesar haircut. I had seen him in the principal's office before, when he and another kid had been suspended for fighting. "I think I know him. He's a senior, right? Football player?"

"Yeah, that's him. She's been dating him for a while. They have a very . . . co-dependent relationship. It's really unhealthy."

"Doesn't seem like she's very happy with him," I said.

"I know." Alice sighed again. "The hard part is making Destiny see that."

Just then a kid came running in to her office, looking anxious. "Miss! Can I talk to you now?" he asked.

"Sorry," she said, beckoning him in as I exited the office. "We'll talk later?"

———————

I was teaching *Animal Farm*. It was first period, and the kids were completely out of it. They were all working quietly, when Destiny raised her hand.

"Miss," she said, in a barely audible voice. "Can I go to the bathroom?"

"Sure, here's the pass." I handed it to her unquestioningly. I was just surprised to see her speaking.

She left the room. I broke the kids into groups, and was in the process of circling between them when Jessica said, "Miss, I really have to go to the bathroom."

"You have to wait until Destiny gets back—she has the pass."

"Uh, Miss, I don't know if you noticed, but Destiny's been gone for fifteen minutes," said another student, Ronald, pointing to his watch.

Shoot. Had it been that long? I peered through the glass window in the door, but I didn't see anyone. So I opened it and stuck my head outside.

There was Destiny. She was leaning against the cinderblock wall, looking up at her boyfriend Anthony. I hadn't considered the aesthetics of her appearance until that moment, and as I looked at her in profile it suddenly struck me that she was a pretty girl—she had honey-blond ringlets tied back in a long pony-tail, fair skin, and light hazel eyes.

Anthony had both palms pressed just above her head on the wall against which she was leaning.

"Destiny," I called to her. She didn't pay attention. "Destiny!"

She turned her face towards me, looking sheepish. "Sorry, Miss."

"Come back to class! Jessica has to use the bathroom . . . she's been waiting for you!"

Languidly, Destiny ducked under Anthony's arms. She walked unhurriedly back into my classroom. From her back pocket, she removed the laminated pass, which was now in the shape of a fruit-rollup. She handed it to Jessica, who ran past me through the doorway.

I cast one more look at Anthony. He narrowed his eyes at me, then turned and sauntered off.

———

Around that time, Anthony started visiting our classroom. I would look up and catch him staring through the glass window in our door. He was clearly looking at Destiny. Sometimes she would look up to see him, and then ask if she could use the bathroom.

"No, you can't go see Anthony," I would tell her. She never argued or reacted much one way or another.

Then sometimes he would stare at her and she would not acknowledge him. I was never sure whether she was unaware of him, then, or if she was intentionally ignoring him.

If he didn't get the desired response, Anthony would wait outside the class until the bell rang, and then squire Destiny off to wherever she went next.

After a few times of this happening, I was already sick of it. I crept over to the door and opened it very quickly. Anthony had not seen me coming, and he looked surprised.

"Step away from the door," I told him. He complied. I stood in the hallway and stared him in the eyes. He was several inches taller than I was. "What class are you supposed to be in right now, Anthony?"

"None—I got a free period."

"Well, that's fine. But I don't like you standing around the door to my classroom like this. Go find something else to do with your time."

"Why?"

"Because you're distracting the students."

"I'm just here for Destiny."

"Doesn't matter. Next time I see you here, I'm calling security. Now scram."

He turned and walked off with that unmistakably cocky swagger. I watched him go. Then, when he was at the end of the hallway, he turned and said to me, "She better not be talking to any other guys, or I'm coming back."

She can talk to whomever she wants, I thought to myself, angry. But he was already around the corner.

I came back into the classroom. Destiny was staring at me, expressionless. I pulled up a chair next to her desk.

"Can we talk for a minute?" I quietly asked her.

She nodded.

"So, I guess you know who I just had a conversation with in the hallway?"

"Anthony," she whispered.

"Yes. He keeps coming around here."

"I know."

"Um . . ." I stalled for a minute, not knowing how to proceed. "Uh, do you really like this guy?"

She shrugged.

"Not really?" I asked hopefully.

She shrugged again.

"Okay, I have to tell you something," I said. "Based on my years and years of expertise with all things boy-related, I have judged your boyfriend to be . . . how can I say this delicately . . . an asshole."

This time, she flashed a small grin.

"You agree."

She nodded.

"Destiny, why are you with him? You could have any other boy you wanted—trust me, they all like you. Anthony—not a good boyfriend. He's *way* too controlling."

"I know." She looked down at her desk.

"Honey . . . you're too good for this. Why don't you break up with him?"

She appraised me with her big, hazel eyes. "Miss," she said quietly, "I don't feel comfortable doing that right now."

I assumed she meant she wanted to break up with him, but was afraid of the repercussions. "Okay. Well, let me know if you need help—anything at all." It was later that night when it occurred to me what she had actually meant: She didn't *want* to leave the relationship.

———

"How are the mice?" I asked Alice, peering through her open door.

She grimaced. "Not so great. I found a dead one right in front of the mini-fridge this morning . . . yuck."

"*Ew*. You're braver than I am." I was chronically unable to remove the little corpses of the ones that died in the traps in my apartment, which despite my best attempts at housekeeping, was constantly under siege from vermin; I would call my next-door neighbor, who did experiments on mice in a lab, to get rid of them for me.

"Eh. Peter wouldn't do it for me," she said, referring to the dean of security. "I wasn't going to sit there working with it in my office." She paused, then gestured towards a beanbag chair. "Wanna come in?"

"Sure." I came in and sat down. She swiveled her computer chair to look at me. I waited a beat and said, "So. Destiny."

"Yes."

"She's one of the ones you see regularly, right?"

She nodded.

"Her boyfriend Anthony is ridiculous," I said. "He's got all the signs of being a future spousal abuser. He cruises by my class every day to make sure she's not talking to any boys. *So* controlling . . ."

"I know. It's awful," Alice sighed.

"Can't her parents do anything about it? Or his?"

"You would think so, right?" she rolled her eyes. "His mother won't admit there's a problem—according to her, Anthony's a perfect angel. As for Destiny, I think her parents want her to get out of it, but they're pretty . . . ineffectual. You know how that is."

I nodded. "But why does she stay with him? Doesn't Destiny get what a jerk he is?"

Alice looked thoughtful for a moment. "She's starting to understand, I think. I'm working on it."

Instantly I felt bad. "I'm sorry. I know you're doing your best. . . ."

"No, it's okay," she said. "It's frustrating to have the situation so out of your control."

———

It was only a short while later that Destiny started coming in with bruises. When I saw them, I smiled ruefully to myself—I had seen this one coming a mile away.

"Destiny. What's going on here?" She was sitting alone again. I touched the bruise on her arm, delicately.

She pulled her arm away. "I fell. In gym."

I wanted to say, "You know that excuse has been used by battered women since biblical times, right?"

Instead I said, "Honey. Please let someone help you. Me, the social worker, any other teacher you trust. You don't deserve this. . . ." I pointed to her arm again.

She made some noncommittal gesture.

Later, I saw her with Anthony in the hallway, their arms wrapped around each other, the very picture of romantic bliss. I could have sworn that he gave me a smug look as I passed by them.

———————

"Can't we just arrest him? Or kick him out of school? Anything!" I cried, pacing around Alice's office.

She smiled. "Based on what? Destiny won't admit that he did it. And it's happening off-campus anyway . . . our reach isn't that far."

Later in the week, I came down a corridor to find Anthony, Destiny, and two school safety officers. They were holding Anthony back, clearly considering arresting him. I turned and went back the way I had come; much as I wanted to see what was happening, I didn't want to get in the way.

"Is Anthony Hall suspended?" I asked Mr. Carver, the principal, later that day.

"Yeah, for a few days . . . it would be better if it were longer," he admitted.

"Seriously. He won't leave Destiny alone."

"Ilana, there's two sides to that story," he told me, looking up from his computer. "I'm not justifying it, what he does to her—but she won't make the choice to leave him either. They're completely co-dependent, and she always goes back to him."

Anthony was gone for a few days, and then, as if to ensure that his girlfriend hadn't cheated on him during his absence, he was back at my door again, peering through the glass.

I looked at Destiny; she was ignoring him.

So I went to the door and stepped into the hall. I looked for security, but couldn't see anyone. *Rats.*

"Anthony. Get away from my door this instant, or I'm calling security."

He smirked at me and looked around the hallway. He knew just as well as I did that even if I called, he still had plenty of time to disappear. "I'm not doing anything," he said.

"Except looking in my door. Go away."

He sneered at me. "I don't like you talking to my girl," he said.

I felt my cheeks getting hot. I wanted for all the world to punch him in the face. Hard. I had never in my life wanted so badly to inflict violence on a student.

I took a deep breath, and then said, in a low voice, "Anthony, you leave here now. And if I have any inkling that you're hitting Destiny again, I will personally make your life a living hell . . . so help me God."

He looked surprised for a moment. Then he said, "You're crazy. You're really crazy." He turned and walked off.

"You bet I am," I said to his back. I came back into the class. Destiny looked at me. I thought I saw her smile.

————

"It's not worth it. Don't risk your teaching career on a kid like that," Alice told me. I had just recounted my interaction with Anthony.

"I just hate him so much," I said, punching the beanbag chair. "You know this isn't just some phase he's going through. He's going to grow up to be an abusive husband, an abusive father, and basically ruin the lives of everyone around him."

"I know. He's despicable. And the sad thing is, he's probably learned all this at home—from his own dad, or some other male relative. Kids don't just come up with this stuff by themselves." She looked at me, and said sternly, "You can't start threatening him, though. That won't help anything, and it will only result in your getting in trouble. Like it or not, he's still a seventeen-year-old. You can't go head-to-head with him."

"So what do I do?" I asked, trying to swallow the lump in my throat.

"You play by the rules. Try to deal with Destiny, rather than with him. You're a good teacher, Ilana. Just keep showing you care—that you will help her, even if she doesn't end up leaving him."

I spent a good month or two following Alice's advice. In first period, I paired Destiny with one of the nicest, smartest girls in the class, Martha. I felt Martha was a perfect choice, because despite her academic savvy, she had come to me with a pregnancy scare earlier that year—she wasn't too goody two-shoes for Destiny to have anything in common with. Privately, I instructed Martha to try and help Destiny as much as she could and to befriend her if possible.

It worked wonderfully. Martha was tremendously patient, a born teacher herself: As soon as I gave an assignment, Martha would scoot her desk up next to Destiny's, explain everything, and then they would work companionably, if quietly, side by side. I would watch them from afar. One time I even saw Destiny giggling at something Martha had said. After a few successive good marks, Destiny's grades started going up, and I could tell she was gaining more confidence. To top it off, my ill-advised threat to Anthony seemed to have done its job—he hadn't been cruising around the hallway by my classroom in a while.

I couldn't have been more thrilled, which is probably why that was the moment everything went wrong.

I was in the teacher's lounge calculating marking period grades when the gym teacher said, "Well, so much for Destiny."

"What do you mean?"

"Her pregnancy—she has this note saying she can't participate in gym."

"What?!"

The gym teacher looked embarrassed. "Oh, no. I thought everyone knew! She came in with a note and everything . . . she asked me to sign it . . . shoot. Don't tell anyone that I told you!"

My first instinct was to go to Destiny directly, pull her out of class, and say, "Tell me it's not true!" But that clearly wasn't a good course of action, I realized. So I waited until she came into class the next day.

I sidled up to her desk and asked, "Destiny, is everything okay?"

"Yeah." She looked at me quizzically.

"Okay, so, is there anything you want to talk about?"

"No . . . Miss, why are you looking at me like that?"

I couldn't get anything out of her. So I let it be—I kept her working with Martha and remained watchful from afar. Within a month or so,

Destiny was starting to show, and I heard students talking about it in the hall, so it seemed safe to acknowledge the pink elephant in the room.

"So, when's the baby due?" I asked her one morning, trying to seem as though it were perfectly natural to bring this up, like it was something we had been talking about all along.

She grinned at my attempt at subtlety. "August, Miss."

"Do you feel ready to be a mom?"

"Yeah . . . my parents are really supportive, and they're going to help me raise it, so I think I'll be fine."

"Well, I'm really glad to hear your parents are helping you through this."

Neither of us mentioned Anthony.

————

Around the end of the term, all the teachers were holding review sessions for finals and Regents exams. The review sessions were not mandatory, so not all the kids came. In a way this was good, because it meant the ones who did show up got plenty of one-on-one attention.

One morning I showed up early. The kids were not yet due in, but a few of them, also early, were sitting around with the history teacher across the hallway. I wandered into the room to find Destiny being consoled by the history teacher, a middle-aged, motherly woman. Anthony and some other kids were sitting around on the desks.

"Anthony," the history teacher was saying, "I think Destiny would feel a lot better if you went to this appointment with her."

"Nawww, man, I got shit to do," he said. "She's always wanting me to do something for her."

"Well, I think you have to take responsibility for that, since it's your child she's pregnant with," the history teacher said, with more patience than I could ever have mustered under the circumstances.

"Yo, I gotta go to my job. Then I can put gas in my car."

I interjected, "What about taking care of the mother of your child?"

His tone turned defensive. "I don't got that much money, and she always wants me to spend it on her. When I get paid, man, I ain't spending *shit* on her. I'm getting gas in the car, and a new iPod." He turned to his friends for approval. They looked confused. "Man," he continued, "During the year, I'm getting a job on Fridays. That way I can work three days a week, and have mad money. And I'm not spending it on *you*," he said, turning suddenly to Destiny.

"Your priorities are completely out of line," I said acidly. "Also, you have class on Fridays. I don't know how you think you'll be able to have any kind of job then . . . but you're mistaken."

"Shut up," he said to me. "You don't know what you're talking about."

I was too stunned to reply. In the history teacher's arms, Destiny continued to cry.

"Anthony," the history teacher said, "Can you please consider how Destiny feels? She must be very scared, going for this appointment all by herself. Don't you think she would feel better if you came with her?"

"Shit, that bitch is always wanting something," Anthony said, heading out. "I got important things to do." He slammed the door behind him.

The history teacher turned to Destiny. "Listen to me, sweetheart. This is what you need to do. Make sure you get his name on the birth certificate, and then you can sue his ass for child-support later on. Trust me, I know what I'm talking about." She grinned ruefully.

Destiny sniffled and nodded.

Later, the history teacher and I were talking. "He's an ass," she said. "But he's got football recruitment scholarships coming in . . . in a way I think it would be better for Destiny, because then he would just leave her alone."

I had trouble seeing it that way—he had effectively ruined Destiny's life, or at least severely limited its possibility, and now here he was getting rewarded with a scholarship.

Destiny didn't show up to my review session on any of the days it was offered. At one point, I found her in the hall waiting for a science review session. "Girl, what's up? Why didn't I see you this morning?" I asked her.

Destiny sighed. "Anthony doesn't want me to be talking to you anymore, Miss," she told me. She seemed vaguely apologetic, but matter-of-fact; this was the situation. There was nothing to be done.

I nodded at her. "Well, I'm always here if you need me."

"What can you do?" Alice told me, as I sat in her office for what would be one of the last times that term. "You can't save them all. You tried. Give yourself a break."

I picked at the colored beanbag chair.

————————

In another review session, Ronald suddenly jumped out of his desk and shoved it away from himself, as if the desk itself were on fire. It clattered noisily across the room, crashing into other desks. Like dominos, the other kids immediately started jumping out of their desks and screaming.

"Ahhhh! Oh my god! Oh my god!" they yelled, standing on their desks.

Instantly freaked out, but without knowing of what, I jumped onto mine. "Jesus Christ, Ronald! What the hell happened?" I screamed, over the cacophony.

"It's a mouse miss! I swear! It just ran through here!"

"What? Where?"

"There—out from under the radiator, then under my desk, and then across the room!"

"Eeeeewww!!!" I cried. This prompted several of the girls to start screaming anew.

"Oh my god!" I yelled, pressing my hands over my ears, and trying to slow down my heart rate. "Stop yelling! Please! I have to think. . . ."

The kids continued screaming and jumping on desks, and I stood on top of mine, frozen. Should I have chased the mouse? Would it come back? Was it my job to deal with this, too? Eventually, I came to.

"Alright, alright, everyone's had their screams, now let's all sit down and finish reviewing," I said, forcing calmness.

"What if it comes back in? Ugh! I can't deal with mice," one of the girls said.

"It won't. Trust me."

"How do you know?"

I pointed at the floor. "Because. You guys have been screaming at the top of your lungs for five minutes straight, and mice don't like loud noises . . . their ears can't tolerate them. They want a quiet situation, where everything is safe and in their control, and nothing big is threatening them. . . ." I paused. I was nearly hyperventilating. My student was looking at me strangely. After a second, she patted me on the shoulder.

"Miss," she said, "You're thinking a little too hard about this."

———

In the middle of a stack of Regents exams that I was grading, I picked up one test. I looked at the name: Anthony Hall.

I wanted so badly to flunk him.

He got a 58. It qualified him for some sort of local diploma, for which you only needed 55. He would graduate and leave at the end of the year.

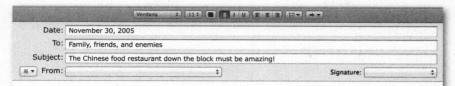

Date: November 30, 2005

To: Family, friends, and enemies

Subject: The Chinese food restaurant down the block must be amazing!

From: [   ]   Signature: [   ]

I am finding it enjoyable to teach these students because many of them actually do the reading. Granted, their average reading-level is low compared to students in many upper-middle-class high schools; the book *To Kill a Mockingbird*, which we just finished, was difficult for them in that it contained a lot of words they did not know (for which I then made them look up definitions and take vocabulary quizzes), although the majority enjoyed it towards the end.

Despite academics being taken more seriously here, no day is short of reminders that I'm teaching in an inner-city school. This past week, for instance, one of the students in my after-school English class (for kids who need to make up the credit) was absent. This is a student who is *always* in and out of trouble—she has a terrible temper, curses out teachers, fights with fists, and has come close to expulsion from the program numerous times. (For some reason she never gives me a problem—but I think this has less to do with our personal relationship, and more to do with the fact that I only teach her two days a week.)

When she came in the next day, the administration informed me that she and some other students had been involved in a fight at the Chinese restaurant down the block from the school. The fight got serious, weapons were drawn, and the student recounted to me that a loaded gun was put to her temple. Everyone involved is apparently standing trial now. I have to write a note to a judge on behalf of this student saying that she is well-behaved in my class, does her work, etc. Then, I believe they are going to give her a "safety transfer" to some other public school, which is what they do if you get jumped one too many times, or have other types of trouble in the geographic area where the school is located.

I will sort of miss this kid, because she is usually friendly with me and we have no problems—but she's caused so much trouble in this school that a safety transfer is probably good.

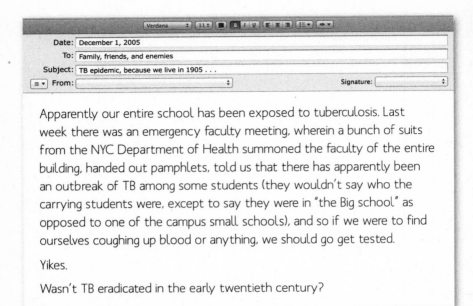

Date: December 1, 2005
To: Family, friends, and enemies
Subject: TB epidemic, because we live in 1905 . . .
From:
Signature:

Apparently our entire school has been exposed to tuberculosis. Last week there was an emergency faculty meeting, wherein a bunch of suits from the NYC Department of Health summoned the faculty of the entire building, handed out pamphlets, told us that there has apparently been an outbreak of TB among some students (they wouldn't say who the carrying students were, except to say they were in "the Big school" as opposed to one of the campus small schools), and so if we were to find ourselves coughing up blood or anything, we should go get tested.

Yikes.

Wasn't TB eradicated in the early twentieth century?

CHAPTER TWELVE

Tyler

"Holy shit, that girl is fine," Tyler whispered to me, sitting on the front of my desk and swinging his legs. He was staring at Jade, one of the girls in my eleventh-grade English class. She was ostensibly doing group work, but in truth was gossiping, blissfully unaware of Tyler's existence.

I didn't actually teach Tyler at this time of day, but he hated his math class and thus would appear in my room during that period several times a week. I would try in vain to send him back to math, reminding him of all the important things he might be missing.

"Seriously, Miss. It's either here, or I'm cruising the hallways," Tyler would say.

Now, he continued to ogle Jade from his perch on my desk. She was gesturing animatedly at her friends and clearly saying something amusing since they were all giggling wildly.

"You and Jade together? I could see that," I said, grinning at the image. Jade, a basketball player, was about five feet, eight inches. I doubted Tyler, at fourteen, was even five feet tall. Still, he would swagger down the hallway, flexing his admittedly impressive muscles at anyone who looked in his direction. I secretly found him adorable.

"Oh my god, Miss, just leave us in a room together for five minutes, and I promise, something's gonna go down," he said with an exaggerated wink.

I swatted at him with my attendance folder. "Big talker! So you need an introduction here, or what?"

He looked horrified. "No, chill! You'll make it mad awkward!"

"True," I conceded. "Well, let me know if you change your mind— you guys would be a cute couple!"

"Miss, any shorty's cute with sexy Tyler by her side!" He grinned impishly at me, then rolled up his sleeve and flexed his bicep.

————

Ironically, I first met Tyler when I was the one teaching his math class— back when he still attended. He was thirteen. He came with a side-kick, Shawn, also thirteen. I was told they were the two youngest (and, noticeably, shortest) kids in the school, having been skipped sometime in elementary school due to impressive test scores.

Most of the ninth-grade boys were still pretty small; they wouldn't hit their growth spurts until tenth or eleventh grade, at which point I would greet them in September to find that they towered over me. But it wasn't just Shawn and Tyler's stature that distinguished them. Both boys, Tyler especially, had a certain round, open-faced aspect that one associates with young children. For the most part, I was used to hulking teenage boys, or at least gawky, acne-ridden adolescents. The two of them seemed like an entirely different species.

Shawn was quiet, but you couldn't miss Tyler if you tried. He was one of the most sociable and confident freshmen I ever met, introducing himself even to teachers whose classes he didn't have, and befriending students in all four grades. Moreover, it quickly became apparent that both of them had already learned every single thing I was teaching their math class. It was the Friday before Halloween, and half the student body was staying home to avoid fallout from the Bloods and Crips initiation that took place annually on October 31. The rites of the initiation were rumored to involve anything from pelting kids with rotten eggs to cutting total strangers with switchblades, and so despite the extra police force that were assigned to our school that day, attendance was low.

To the half of the class who had shown up, I gave out a "holiday math challenge." I had one for every holiday. This one was a permutation problem—the object was to calculate the number of different orders in which one could trick-or-treat at a given set of houses.

"If you figure this out, you get candy," I said, holding up a bag of Reese's Peanut-Butter Cups. "Now work in pairs, and remember, when you get your answer, don't tell anyone!"

I began to pass out the papers. Bribery always worked well, and the kids who received their papers first got right to work. I wasn't even halfway through distributing the papers when I heard a high-pitched "Yes!" across the room, followed by the unmistakable slap of a high-five.

"Miss! It's 120! We got it! We got it!" Tyler cried, jumping up and down and waving his paper in the air. Beside him, Shawn smirked.

"Punk! I mean . . . sorry. Tyler!" As I spoke, I could already see the other kids scrambling to write down "120" on their papers. So much for group work. "Didn't I just say not to tell anyone?"

"Oh yeahhhhhh!" He had a momentary look of dawning comprehension and then yelled, "Yo! Just kidding, people! It was . . . 83!"

I told the assistant principal that I thought Shawn and Tyler should be moved up. She nodded, said she would look into it, and promptly forgot. I'm not sure whether this was because she was so busy, or because I didn't have any credibility as a math teacher; the original person slated for the job had left on day two after some students threw a stapler at her head, and I'd been given the position because I had some math classes under my belt from college. I was a stop-gap, in place only until a better solution could be found.

I kind of felt bad for the kids who had me; as a math teacher, I wasn't exactly sure what I was doing.

So I attempted to compensate for this, at least where Tyler and Shawn were concerned. After school, when the two of them would invariably come wandering into my classroom, begging me to give them candy or write a note that would get them out of Football Study Hall, I would teach them new concepts and give them more high-level problems to solve. We called it "challenge math."

I thought it was a pretty good arrangement until an outside consultant "math coach" came and sat in on my lesson. I was lecturing about variables, and writing problems on the board. The majority of the kids, having already been bribed, were feigning polite interest in the value of "x" when "y" was equal to four.

Presently, a paper football hit the side of my head.

"Oops! Sorry, Miss!" Tyler called. Then I heard a loud stage whisper: "Yo, Shawn, learn how to catch!" But it was too late—they had attracted the attention of the math coach, who sailed across the room and started interrogating the two of them about the contents of their math folders.

"They shouldn't be in this class," he told me afterwards. "I'm going to see to it that they get moved up." Both their names were removed from my attendance roster within forty-eight hours. I marveled at how fast you could get your roster changed when you *weren't* a teacher.

––––––––

Parent-teacher conferences took place on a Thursday night in late fall. One of the awkward parts of the event was that, at best, only a third of the parents ever showed up—and they usually weren't the ones you wanted to speak to anyway. Another awkward part was that the parents brought their children with them, sometimes with younger brothers or sisters in tow. It was difficult to critique a student's performance in the class when the student in question—surrounded by several siblings— was seated right in front of you.

"I have bad news: I'm afraid Charlene is failing math," I told one parent, angling my grade book towards her to reveal that her daughter had turned in no homework and failed every single test.

Without missing a beat, the woman turned to Charlene, who was sitting glumly next to her, and slapped her across the face.

"Stop it! Don't hit Charlene!" I cried, louder than I meant to. "Hitting her won't help her to pass math!"

The mother glared at Charlene. Charlene, in turn, glared at me. I wished for a hole to crawl into and thought glumly that Charlene would probably never show up to my math class again.

Toward the end of the evening, I was standing by the door to my classroom scanning the emptying hallway when Tyler and his mother came by.

"Tyler!" I said, genuinely glad to see him. When he hugged me, his little shaved head only came up to my chin. I shook his mother's hand.

"Miss Garon? Do you have any . . . candy?" he asked, peering eagerly behind my back and into the classroom.

"Not now, baby," Tyler's mother told him. She was a dignified, middle-aged woman with a well-cut brown suit, spectacle glasses, and a bun. It turned out she was a teacher as well—fourth grade, she told me. She and her husband were very invested in Tyler's education. We stood at the doorway and talked shop for a few minutes while Tyler played a videogame he had brought with him.

Compared to a lot of these kids, Tyler was lucky. He had two parents. They cared about whether he passed his classes. His mother didn't seem inclined to hit him, at least not in public.

"We wish he could have stayed in your class instead of going up to tenth-grade math," his mother said. Tyler was still absorbed in his videogame and seemed to be ignoring us.

"But it's good that he can have a more challenging curriculum now."

"I know," his mother said. She furrowed her brow. "But compared to the students in this new class, he's *so* young . . . his teacher says he acts up. He's just not mature enough to be with the tenth-graders. I wonder if he wouldn't have done better just staying put."

––––––––

As it turned out, his mother was right. Tyler got kicked out of math class several days in a row. After that, as far as I could tell, he stopped going altogether. He would come to my room instead, and press his little face against the glass window of my closed door, peering in plaintively.

"Awww, it's baby Tyler!" the girls in my eleventh-grade class would coo almost in unison, or "Oh, he's mad cute—he looks like Kermit the frog!" I didn't quite see the resemblance. "Let him come in, Miss—he's sad!"

So I would open the door, and Tyler would bound into the room, sit down at my desk, and wait to be made useful. The first few times he showed up, I denied him entrance, begging him to go back to math or threatening to call his mother. It didn't work; he'd leave that day, but would reappear at my door twenty-four hours later. If I mistakenly left the classroom door unlocked, I would turn around to find Tyler seated in one of the desks, having quietly snuck in and now trying to blend in with the rest of my students.

I gave up trying to kick him out—I just didn't have the heart to do it so many times. When I had materials to sort or distribute, I made him my personal assistant. Otherwise, I would give him a pen and instruct him to do his homework quietly.

Midway through the year, I knew he wasn't doing well. In the beginning of the term, Tyler had been pulling a 90 average—I had seen his first report card. Now, the names of students who had made the Dean's List were posted outside the principal's office. Students who made at least an 80 average were eligible. Shawn was near the bottom.

Tyler's name wasn't on the list.

———

My second chance with Tyler came the following September, when I found him on my roster again—for tenth-grade English. This time, he had been separated from Shawn, apparently at the behest of both of their parents. The extra year had given him some height—he was now nearly as tall as I was—but he had maintained the same open, doe-eyed expression that had endeared him to me in the first place.

His behavior was less endearing. I would pass him in the hallway with his arm around one of a rotation of girls he was apparently seeing, and he would wink at me conspiratorially. In class, he was chatty, constantly yelling at his friends across the room, getting up out of his seat to go visit with his latest romantic conquest, and generally causing a ruckus.

"Tyler, come on!" I said, after I caught him standing across the room from his partner during pair work, discussing the previous weekend's game with one of his fellow JV football players.

"Awww, Miss! I'm done already! Just one more second," he begged, as he leaned back down to chat with his friend.

I looked across the room at his work partner, Gerard, who sat at his desk with his chin in his palm, looking irritated. Gerard was a sweet, motivated kid, unapologetically nerdy—all of my conversations with him somehow ended up being on the subject of battleships. I had a hunch that he was doing the work for both of them. Now, I met Gerard's gaze and raised an eyebrow. *Is Tyler done?* Gerard caught my meaning immediately. He shook his head.

I was disappointed. True, Tyler had always been very social. But he seemed to have lost that spark he'd had as a ninth-grader, when he had jumped up and down excitedly upon finding the answer to the challenge math question. Somehow I had assumed that innate intelligence and good parenting would keep him motivated, even when the environment around him wasn't exactly oriented towards academics.

Reluctantly, I called home. His mom answered. "Oh, hi, Ms. Garon. What's he done now?" she said.

I found myself trying to console her. "It's really not all that bad . . . he's so smart . . ." I stammered. "It's just that he really isn't focused. He's so chatty. He just wanders around the class socializing instead of doing the work. He'd be a top student if he could just buckle down. . . ."

"You know, he learned to read when he was four," she told me wearily. "His father and I have spent so much time working with him. This just disappoints us so much—we want him to get a college scholarship, and that won't happen if he keeps carrying on like this. It's tenth grade—he's not in middle school anymore."

———————

The morning after my conversation with his mother, Tyler was livid. He skulked into class and seated himself all the way in the back row. Then he put his head down on the desk. Another student asked him what was wrong, but he ignored her totally.

"Tyler, your seat is in front. Move up please," I said.

Instantly, he sprang up, and shot me a look of pure hatred. I flinched.

"What, you gonna call my house again? Just leave me the hell alone!" he shouted. Then he put his head down on the desk again.

The other kids looked at me questioningly. I inclined my head towards him and motioned "cut" with my hand—*Let him be, guys.* They got the message.

Tyler gave me the silence treatment for the rest of the week, which seemed terribly long. He ignored any attempts I made to address him and rolled his eyes at anything I directed to the entire class. He sat at his desk either with his head down or with his arms crossed, sulking. Periodically, he would utter a sound that I would describe as a "bored noise"—it was sort of an irritated huff—that was a little too loud and pointed to be accidental.

The kids who were chronic discipline problems—the ones who would get suspended constantly, fight in class, curse at teachers, or just walk out spontaneously when they got bored—found Tyler's antics too childish to even bother with. But the "good" kids were interested. I could tell they were torn between their desire to register their admiration at his refusal to participate, by flashing surreptitious grins in his direction that they thought I couldn't see, and their fear of being associated with someone who was being such a badass. The fact that he was, strictly speaking, one of their own—a smart kid who generally wasn't so much "bad" as overly social and loud—made him all the more accessible as an icon of rebellion. By the end of the week, they were all imitating him, putting their heads on the desk and complaining, "Aww, this is mad boring!" regardless of what I told them to do.

It was time to cut my losses. I approached Tyler while the kids were doing group work.

"Can we talk for a minute?"

"Miss, I got nothing to say to you." He angled his face away from me.

"Okay, then just listen. I'm sorry I called your house. I wish I hadn't felt like I had to. But you're being very disruptive. It's hard for me, as your teacher, to conduct class when you're distracting everyone. And when I tell you not to, you don't listen. You just ignore what I say. It makes me feel . . ."—I paused for effect—"very disrespected."

That got his attention. He whipped his head back around, his expression one of surprise.

"Really?"

"Yeah, and the other students really look up to you, so—"

"Miss, I am so sorry," he said. He genuinely looked it, too. "This will never happen again. If you ever have a problem with me, or feel I am disrespecting you in any way, I want you to call this number."

He scrawled ten digits on a piece of notebook paper, ripped it out, and handed it to me.

"It's my cell," he told me.

"So, if I have a problem with you again, you want me to call . . . you."

"Exactly," he said. Then he reached across the desk and gave me a hug.

————

The rest of Tyler's year was unspectacular. His grades went down in every subject, including my own. When calculating his term grades, I found myself looking for excuses to push him up to an 80, just because I hated seeing such a smart kid get such poor grades.

It wasn't like he deserved extra points. Though he was significantly less "disrespectful" to me personally, he showed little interest in any of the work we were doing. His assignments were sloppy, clearly intended to fulfill only the bare minimum requirement, and were usually late to boot.

At one point, the school underwent some sort of evaluation based on an hour-long standardized test that all the tenth-graders were supposed to take. Naturally, the English teachers were told to administer the tests during our forty-five-minute periods, thereby guaranteeing that no student could possibly finish on time.

The kids complained. "Aww, Miss! How they expect us to do this?" they cried.

"Look, just do your best—the school's being evaluated here, not you individually," I told them, hoping it was true.

They got to work, not without the requisite grumbling. The room was quiet. About ten minutes in, Tyler got up from his desk and swaggered towards me, his Scantron® Sheet in hand.

"What's up, big guy? You done?" I whispered.

Tyler grinned. "Check out my paper. It's a present for the test people."

He had neatly bubbled in "F - - - Y O U" in three-inch-high letters on his sheet.

———

Looking back, I can chart how Tyler slipped, each step that separated the lackadaisical student he became from the true scholar he could have been. I know what happened, but I cannot say why with any certainty. Tyler had brains, parents who encouraged good study habits, and a slew of teachers who, had he shown the smallest glimmer of motivation, would have bent over backwards to help him with schoolwork, specialized summer programs, or scholarships. He had so much promise, so many people rooting for him. He should have been our school's great success story.

The only culprits I can identify are shadowy ones: the environment of our school, and the implicit messages of Tyler's peers. Athleticism was universally valued. So was sex appeal. Clowning was rewarded with laughs. Good grades, however, were a double-edged sword—though your teachers and parents might be thrilled, you didn't get any claps on the shoulder from your peers for making straight A's. In fact, they were liable to turn on you, to mock you for your scholarly habits. Even worse, they might accuse you of the ultimate treachery: "acting white."

As a young black kid, Tyler must have understood this reality. He must have figured that if he scraped by on the academic margins, doing the bare minimum, he could ultimately pass his classes while still maintaining the social status he found so alluring.

He prioritized accordingly.

———————

The following year, when I went off to graduate school, the students would occasionally IM me to say hello, report on the results of a soccer game, complain about their teachers, or ask for help with homework.

One night in late spring, Tyler popped up on my computer screen.

"Hey Miss. What's up? I'm applying for a job at Target . . . can you recommend me? All you have to do is tell them I did really great in your class," he typed.

In fact, he had barely pulled a 70 in my class. Furthermore, I knew from the guidance counselor, with whom I was still friendly, that Tyler's grades had continued to go down since my departure. He had all his credits, she told me, but just that—he'd be lucky to get into a community college.

"It's a shame," she told me. "He's so intelligent . . . but he's lazy as can be."

In my mind's eye, I still saw the thirteen-year-old math whiz who wanted candy and admission to my classroom. I had never had the heart to say no to that kid—for better, or for worse.

"Of course I'll recommend you," I told him.

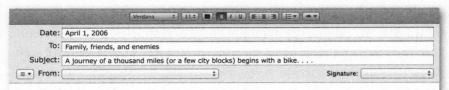

Date: April 1, 2006
To: Family, friends, and enemies
Subject: A journey of a thousand miles (or a few city blocks) begins with a bike. . . .
From:
Signature:

Sometimes I feel depressed about the difficult situations that my students encounter on a daily basis: During the recent NYC transit strike, for instance, some resourceful young men in my English class formed a "bike club" so that they could ride to school together. The impetus for organizing this little group was to avoid getting "jumped" by thugs who would have found it amusing to hurt them and steal their bicycles. It makes me angry that these teens could not even ride their bikes to school in broad daylight without considering the need for an armed escort. But as the kids pointed out to me, the Bronx is that kind of place.

And yet, through this, they flourish. I got back from Boston this afternoon, where the top thirty students and I (along with nine other chaperones) have been visiting Boston University, Northeastern, and Harvard. These highly motivated kids (among them, all the members of the bike club) have been working steadily throughout the last three years. Graduation is a realistic goal for them, and there is hope that they might be able to attend college. Certainly they will require huge amounts of support, financial and otherwise, but as we've told them, there are scholarships out there for tough, smart, inner-city kids.

It was a joyful experience to walk around the campuses with them. Some of these kids have never been out of New York save for occasional trips home to the Dominican Republic; they were wide-eyed and delighted by the green and open spaces of the Boston Public Gardens, as well as the mix of historic and modern buildings that dot the city.

It is these bright spots, such as touring Boston with this promising group of kids who wouldn't stop taking photos with their camera phones, that make me stay in this tough school, that reinforce for me (when I am doubting it) that I have made the right decision by choosing a "socially responsible" career over one that would make it easier to afford my rent.

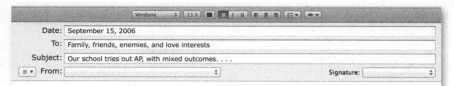

Date: September 15, 2006
To: Family, friends, enemies, and love interests
Subject: Our school tries out AP, with mixed outcomes. . . .
From: Signature:

This year I am teaching four sections of tenth-grade English and one section of twelfth-grade advanced placement (AP). The AP class is my special project. Last spring I told the principal that I thought the school's main hope of legitimacy lay in offering some classes that would make its students competitive in college applications. I urged him to start an AP program in our school, which should have included a variety of courses.

As it happened, AP English was the only course that materialized, and (as I hoped he would) the principal offered it to me. I went to the AP training course this summer in Virginia to become certified and am now piloting our school's fledgling AP program.

So. The class was to be capped at twenty. I hand-selected the top twenty students at the end of last year, based on their performance in my English class. I told these twenty students that they were going to be in AP. They were very excited.

I ordered books for twenty students. In mid-July, I stamped and posted summer reading assignments (from my home) to these twenty students. So imagine my surprise when I come into class the first day and there are twenty-seven kids on the roster.

This is by no means the end of the world, but it is frustrating. The point of keeping AP small was so that the students could get a lot of individual attention in their preparation for the exam and college. It is far more difficult to do that with twenty-seven students. Also, the seven new ones have not read the summer reading book (How could they have? No one even told them they were taking the class until last week!), and so everyone is on a different schedule.

Plus, I am five books short for every novel we're going to read this year. Let that be a lesson to me: never order only two extra copies in a class set.

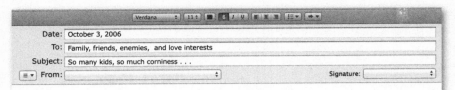

There are 112 tenth-graders in our school, and I teach English to every one of them. I am still getting new students virtually every single day, and we are already at the end of the second week of school. I have never in my life taught this many students at once. Usually I have the same number of classes, but I'll have an advisory or something, where I get a repeat of the same students I had earlier in the day.

Also, in "Big Explorers," my previous school, I easily had that many kids on my roster—but they would never show up.

The tenth-grade class came to me with a reputation for wild behavior. The teacher who had them last year balked at the prospect of dealing with them again, and so I took them off her hands (feeling gracious because I'd been given my special AP course . . . silly me). And I have to say that so far, they are everything I've expected, and more. Mostly, they are rambunctious . . . they jump out of their seats constantly, wander around the class without permission, and scream at their peers across the room. It is like having a class of thirty-three hyperactive five-year-olds, except these kids are sixteen. An alphabetical seating arrangement and threats to call parents did little to calm them, and so I have resorted to my favorite pedagogical method: publicly deriding their ability to shoot baskets and impress girls. It has mixed results.

At one point, during a particularly tiresome argument with one student, in which he was refusing to move himself to the front of the room, I finally said, "Look at me. This is not a democracy. This is a teach-ocracy. I'm in charge. Now get your rear end to the front, stat!" The students roared. Then one said "Hey, wait, that was corny!" and the rest decided it was corny, as well, and the ensuing discussion of my relative corniness ("Mr. Carver is even cornier, yo!") lasted several minutes until I managed to threaten enough students with calls to home to make the majority of the class calm down.

YEAR 4

CHAPTER THIRTEEN

Benny & Mo

"I don't care what anyone tells me—they are the worst tenth-grade class I've ever taught!" I yelled, enthusiastically releasing a day's pent-up frustration now that we were outdoors. Dan, a science teacher who had all the same students as I did, and I were walking to the subway; he always walked with me up to the station after school before continuing on to catch the Bx12 bus down the road. "I can't deal with it—I've never had such a misbehaving class!"

He volleyed it right back. "I know! What the hell! Try teaching them science—I'm afraid to have them in the lab because they just destroy all the breakable stuff and set things on fire!"

"They don't take anything seriously!" I fumed. "I gave them an assignment, to design an island for *Lord of the Flies*, and those boys—you know, the group Lawrence is the ringleader of—they made an island that had mountains all around the outside and a big hole in the center, and they called it 'Vagina-land'!"

That did it. We both burst out laughing.

"Alright, dear, I'll see you tomorrow," I said after we hugged each other. I turned and stepped into the crosswalk.

I heard a loud screech as a car hit me. I tumbled over the edge of its hood, and then landed on my side in the middle of the crosswalk.

I lay on the asphalt, looking at the tires of the car, which were now eye-level. The wind had been knocked out of me. Everything was quiet. Then I heard Dan yelling.

"Ilana! Are you okay!?"

"Yes, I'm fine!" I yelled back. My voice had little force since the wind had been knocked out of me. I picked my torso up to show that I could and waved at Dan. "I'm okay . . . my leg just hurts!" I motioned as if to move.

"Ilana! Don't you f—ing move from that spot!" yelled Dan. He and another man, a construction worker in an orange vest who had been working nearby, came to the middle of the street. They helped me up and over to the curb, where they set me down on the grass.

The driver of the car came over to me. By now a crowd had gathered. Behind him, I could see his car—a gray, '80s-model Toyota. The door had been left open, and it was parked in the middle of the street.

"Hey, I'm sorry—I just didn't see you crossing," he said. Later I would be told that he was a young Latino man with close-cropped hair, but to this day I remember nothing of his face.

Everything was throbbing, particularly my leg. I knew I could move, so I figured I wasn't dying.

I needed to tell the driver that it was not his fault. "It's okay, man," I told him. "I should have looked both ways. It's okay." I reached up for his hand and shook it. "It's alright man. I'm okay."

Dan leaned over me and cupped my cheeks in his hands. "Shut up," he whispered in my ear, severely. "You're hurt. You're not thinking clearly. Don't say anything else."

"Oh, Dan!" I cried and started sobbing. Dan looked like he was going to cry, as well. He sat next to me on the ground and held my hands.

Someone had called an ambulance. They came and took my pulse. They put me on a stretcher.

"Where's the guy who hit me?" I asked Dan. I felt inexplicably groggy.

"He drove away," said the construction worker in the orange vest, glancing knowingly at a couple of people around us who groaned. "But don't worry," he said, grinning sardonically. "I got his license number."

At some point I was piled into an ambulance and taken to Jacobi Hospital. I don't remember much of the ride, except that Dan came with me. In the waiting room, a guy who had overdosed on drugs was throwing up on the floor, and a young schizophrenic man had been restrained because he had tried to kill his family, who now waited tearfully beside the stretcher upon which he had been strapped down.

My ailments were comparatively minor. Other than having screwed up the tendons in my knee, I had emerged unscathed. Two hours and several conversations with the police later, I hobbled out of Jacobi with crutches. Dan was at my side, along with my then-boyfriend, Aaron, who had rushed to meet us at the hospital.

We had some trouble hailing a taxi. When a gypsy cab finally slowed down for us, I was relieved.

"Hey Miss," the cabby yelled.

I looked in the cab and realized it was one of my former students. It took me a second to recognize him, but he patiently jogged my memory—"I'm Mohammad. People called me 'Mo,' remember? You taught me that there are really good Jewish people, Miss. I'm Muslim, remember? And I'd never met a Jewish person before you. Now I have a professor who's Jewish, at Bronx Community College, and he's totally amazing! He makes me so interested in learning about marketing. . . ."

He prattled on, happily regaling me with the details of his life. I had to smile. Here I was coming out of the hospital in the middle of the Bronx, and who should pick me up but one of my former students— at that, one who was doing something with his life, educating himself, working, and succeeding.

Mohammad stopped at home because it was Ramadan and he needed to pick up his dinner so he could eat at sundown. I lay back in the cab, tucked between Aaron and Dan, nearly falling asleep under the influence of the pain medication. When he got out of his cab at my house to help me out of the car (despite Dan and Aaron's presence), I tipped him $15 on a $25 fare, kissed both his cheeks, and thanked him for saving me.

The following week I went down to the precinct to file the forms for my police report. They told me they had tracked the license number that the construction worker had taken off the car's plates.

"Unfortunately, that didn't help us," said one of the cops, apologetically. "It's registered to some chick named Maria Lopez, and the address is a parking lot upstate. Totally bogus. That's probably why he drove off so fast."

All the same, they had me look at mug shots to see if I could recognize the guy who hit me. I knew at the outset that I would never be able to, but I tried to give it a fair shake anyway. I clicked through the list of young Latino men, aged eighteen to twenty-eight—the parameters the cops had been given by the bystanders.

I *did* see one familiar face.

"Benny Rodriguez?" I cried out in surprise. I hadn't seen him in three years. He had been the boyfriend of one of my former students, Desi, and would come to my English class even though he wasn't registered for it. Perhaps I would have been more inclined to kick him out if he had not been such an amazing participant—he was always first to volunteer to read aloud, to act, even to write the essays. I had told him multiple times that he was the best student I never had.

The cops near me looked over and chuckled. "Oh, Benny," said one of them. "Let's see what we have him on. . . ." He looked at the screen and then crowed, "Breaking and entering!" And he and his partner laughed and called to the other cops, "Look at that! The teacher found one of her students in the mug shots!"

I thought, "He wasn't exactly my student . . ." But I didn't bother to correct them. I just sat there, thinking. A face appeared in my mind—not Benny's, but the face of the kid who hit me with his car. I couldn't make out the physical details, but I remembered that expression—the anxiety, the confusion. That part was imprinted in my memory, though it would do me no good here.

I had never been angry with him, I realized, because on an unconscious level I had seen kids like Benny in him, kids who were basically cool, and could have turned out just like Mo, were it not for one colossally dumb, life-ruining mistake. He had stood in front of me, frightened, guilty, and unsure what to do. He knew he had f—ed up, and didn't know how to fix it. So, in a panic, he had fled.

I was sure that if Benny had seen an opportunity for escape during his bust for breaking and entering, he would have done the same thing.

I felt dissatisfied, but I do not think that I would have felt any better if I had been able to pick out the mug shot of the guy who hit me from the database instead of my former student's. I collected my books, thanked the officers, and left the precinct. *You win some, you lose some,* I told myself. There would be class in the morning.

Date: November 6, 2006
To: Family, friends, enemies, and love interests
Subject: Phone dates with parents
From: Signature:

I called ten households this week, which really we're supposed to do every week, but I almost never manage to get done. Some of the kids are really out of control with their rudeness and disrespect for authority. I decided to call their houses after one girl repeatedly told me "Move!" when I was in her way. When I said, "Excuse me?" she said, "My name isn't 'excuse me'!" and then muttered "Bitch!" under her breath, I knew it was time.

The mother did not apologize for her daughter's behavior or even suggest that she would reprimand the girl—rather, she implicitly justified it by citing "problems with other girls" as the logical explanation. This is not the first time I've gotten this type of response from parents, and I always find it particularly infuriating (more so, perhaps, than the usual negligence) in that they are enabling their children's patterns of failure by looking for outside excuses and never correcting the problem.

That said: Teaching is one of those things that gets markedly easier with time. I also think that when I can eventually figure out the right seating arrangement, I will have slightly better control over these giant classes. So hopefully I can manage that next week, in between discussions of the perfect murder weapon (we're reading *Julius Caesar*) and making the twelfth graders listen to U2 and Rufus Wainwright during group work. Hell, no one ever said I wasn't "mad corny". . . .

CHAPTER FOURTEEN

Tonya

My cell phone rang while I was shopping for tea in Fairway, an eclectic grocery on Seventy-Fourth Street, a year and a half after I had left teaching to go to graduate school. The phone number wasn't one I recognized.

"Who is this, please?"

"Miss, it's Tonya!" my former student announced joyfully. "How's it going?"

Tonya. I had heard from her only sporadically since I had started graduate school, and she, college. A tiny, beautiful, effervescent black girl with long cornrow braids, she had been best friends with Adam, and herself one of the top students in the small school where I had taught. She was bright and talented, with a 92 grade-point average and consistent participation in youth theater programs, all of which had eventually garnered her a full scholarship to an upstate private school.

Despite these accomplishments, Tonya suffered from deep self-doubt where her relationships with men were concerned. When I was her English teacher, she would come talk to me about various boys for hours after school ended—analyzing their every comment or action. "You *know* he loves me," she would insist, when I would question any of their intentions. She would leave only when I finally did.

Her father was absent, and I always worried that she was trying to recapture that lost love in every boy she met (boys who, I always felt, were undeserving and unappreciative of her awesomeness). When she got into a relationship, I noticed, things would become physical quickly; she would immediately regret it, but then do it again with someone new a couple of months later.

In truth, the behavior of "hooking up" a lot was not uncommon for girls Tonya's age, in any area—when I was tutoring kids in a wealthy suburban area of Westchester, their accounts of weekend activities were punctuated with similar stories. But Tonya was uncommonly sensitive. Each time she was spurned by one of the guys with whom she'd gotten involved, it seemed like that rejection bored into an ever-growing hole in her.

"I wish I hadn't done it," she told me once, referring to a boy in her grade. "It makes me feel bad now." She was perched on top of the desk in my empty classroom. I was in the rear of the room, shelving books.

"Why do you think you feel bad?" I asked her, not turning from my closet.

"I don't know. I just wish I hadn't."

"Were you 'into it' at the time?" No response. "Did he pressure you?"

"Not really. I mean . . . I knew he wanted to, but he didn't force me or anything."

"What made you feel you had to do it, then?" I was conscious to keep my voice as neutral as possible.

"I don't know."

I sat down across from her. "Do you want to know what I think? I think you hooked up with him because you felt it would make him emotionally closer to you. And you wanted that closeness. But it doesn't really work like that. . . ."

"That's stupid!" she interrupted, her eyes flaring at me.

I knew I was on thin ice; my amateur psychology tended to have mixed results. "But Tonya . . . why is it stupid?" I persisted. "Why are you ashamed that, like any of us, you just want to be loved?"

"Shut up! I hate you! You don't know anything about me!" she screamed. She jumped off the desk and sprinted out the classroom door, slamming it behind her, leaving me more unsettled than I wanted to admit.

Tonya ignored me completely for two days. Then she came to me after class at the end of the week. "I'm ready for you to apologize," she announced.

"Hon, I'm sorry your feelings are hurt, but I think the reason you're upset is because you know what I said has a kernel of truth to it."

She looked like she was about to argue with me, but then she stopped. "You have a lot to learn about young people!" she told me, mustering some venom. Then she seemed to give up and spent the next twenty minutes regaling me with the details of a humorous incident that had taken place in her chemistry class.

That tended to be our relationship—disclosure from her, attempts at advice from me, followed by the silent treatment, and then a reunion. It was exhausting sometimes. During winter vacation of her senior year, I awoke one morning to find a message on my cell phone: "Ms. Garon— it's Tonya. Angel and I took it to the next level. We didn't use protection. Don't call back. Bye." After a couple of moments of confusion, I remembered that "Angel" was a twenty-five-year-old (the same age I was) whom she had met at her job. I tried to call her despite her orders. Her ringer was off.

So now, standing in the tea aisle at Fairway nearly two years later, I wondered what bomb she was about to drop. As it turned out, her call was benign. "I'm writing a poem for class," she said. "It's about a boy I like. But I think something is missing. Can I email it to you?"

I read her poem in the privacy of my bedroom that night:

The touching of your face brings a certain intimacy you never heard of. It's like getting your palm read by a psychic. . . .

I need to feel your face so that I can feel as special as I am suppose to feel.

Like I am a part of that exclusive country club that everyone wants to join, 'cause of the beautiful people and expensive water, even though I don't play golf.

I read the last line about the country club, cracked up, and then instantly hated myself for finding humor in what was clearly an emotional outpouring. What kind of teacher was I?

"Hon," I said to her on the phone when I called to give her feedback. "I think what your poem needs is . . . well . . . more risk."

"Risk? Like, how?"

"Well, we have this 'ode to a boy' here—but your reader doesn't really know what the stakes are. Does he love you back? Is he going to reject you? How would you feel if you lost him?"

"Those are stupid suggestions," she told me, laughing.

"Well sor-*ry*, missy! You asked my opinion, remember? Take it or leave it."

"I'm just not going to write about my feelings," she said, suddenly severe.

Ah. So we were at this point again.

"Tonya, that's your prerogative—but I think poetry has to be at least somewhat about your feelings. You said something's missing, and that's what it is."

"Ugh, forget it! I'm not turning in this poem after all! Good*night!*" she said, slamming down the phone.

I went to bed feeling frustrated. By the time I got up in the morning, I already had two messages on my cell phone, which had been turned to silent.

The first one said, "Miss Garon, it's Tonya. I'm turning in that poem I wrote senior year of high school, about how my mom's house smells like popcorn. I'm not writing anything emotional. Okay, bye."

I deleted it, and went on to the second message. "It's me again. Tonya. You know what? I realized I hate that boy from the poem! And I'm so angry I can't even think straight! I hate him so much! That's why I can't write the damn poem! I'm furious!" *Click.*

I was about to call her back, but I stopped myself. *She's nineteen*, I told myself. *She's got to figure this out for herself.*

In subsequent years, she would prove more than capable: She would graduate from college and go on to get an MFA in poetry, becoming one of our small school's first students to get a graduate degree. She would leave the east coast, meet new people, and fulfill every expectation I or anyone else could ever have had of her. But neither of us could know that yet. And right now, as I stood there holding my cell phone in my hand, I felt we'd come to a make-or-break moment wherein it was crucial for each of us to disentangle from the other.

You can't keep going there with her forever.

So instead, I wrote her a short email. "Sorry you're having a tough time," I told her. "You're strong. I know you will be okay."

I put the phone on vibrate in case she called back. Then I went into the kitchen to make some tea. It seemed like the only sure thing to do.

CHAPTER FIFTEEN

Callum

Another teacher once described Callum, one of my eleventh-grade students, as "the most brilliant dumbass I've ever met." I think he meant it the other way around: Callum was one of those kids who had a sort of white-hot intelligence—he'd remember everything you said, no matter how long ago, and offer the most pithy, insightful analysis of any topic—but then would be several days late turning in the essay at the end of term. As a result, when I met Callum, he was a solid B-student, despite his capability of explaining topics of theoretical physics to me during his study hall period. His classmates called him "The Professor."

A tall, very lean, handsome young man with cornrows and just a hint of a moustache, Callum appealed to a certain type of girl—usually the smart, quirky, "alternative" types who shared his interests in anime (really, anything involving "Japanimation") and drawing, which he was decently good at. He was quiet, but not shy, and did not suffer fools gladly: Once, when the school's top football player spontaneously jumped up on a desk and started flexing his muscles, for which the principal (who happened to be passing by) immediately gave him lunch detention, Callum rolled his eyes and looked my way. "Infantile," he muttered, just loud enough for me to hear. The trace of a Jamaican accent was evident only from the precise way he emphasized some of his consonants.

"Have you ever noticed," he said once in class, during a discussion of politics which was, naturally, dominated by the extreme liberal bent of the northeast, "that people who are very liberal are at one end of the spectrum, and people who are very conservative are at the other—but really they're not so dissimilar in their thinking, even if their principles are different? So basically, extremes are the same, and a continuum is really . . . more of a circle." Then he chuckled to himself, as if someone had made a joke earlier that he had just gotten.

Days later, in typical fashion, he failed to turn in a paper. In response, I threatened—in the most professional way possible—to beat him up.

He burst out laughing and turned in the paper the next day.

———

Callum was sixteen when I was his teacher, and I was twenty-four. From the beginning, our affinity for each other—not just as student and teacher, but simply as people—was evident. We had identical taste in nerdy media; I lent him my copy of *Freakonomics*, and he introduced me to "anti-folk" singer-songwriter Regina Spektor. During his study hall period, he would position his student-sized desk near my teacher-sized desk, so as to sidetrack me from my vain attempts to update my grade book with conversations about the movie *Donnie Darko* or proposed resolutions to the political tensions in the Middle East.

"If you weren't my teacher, we'd hang out on the weekends," he told me once. I couldn't help but agree.

Once, we were so immersed in a discussion about the TV show *House* and its connection to Sherlock Holmes that his classmate Adam came up to us, listened for a moment, and then said, "Yeah, I'll just let you guys be."

———

It was strange for me to be so "in sync" with a student. Though I was certainly closer in age to the kids than I was to many of the faculty members, in most cases there still would have been an unbridgeable divide between us, and rightfully so—I was the teacher, and they were the students. I was (with minimal success) the disciplinarian in the room, and they were the somewhat unwilling beneficiaries of my attempts at classroom management.

Part of the reason for Callum's and my friendly rapport was that I never needed to discipline him. In spite of his propensity for turning in assignments late, if at all, Callum was one of the best students I ever had. He was always interested in the material, always engaged, always performing well on tests (despite never studying), always contributing brilliantly to class discussions; I never once had to correct his behavior in any way, and if I had, I suspect he'd have been more shocked and disappointed than I. Though discipline was undeniably part of my job (an aspect that I have never been quite able to get behind; at that time I stubbornly insisted that I'd become a high school teacher, as opposed to elementary school, to avoid having to punish kids), Callum saw no reason it should have had to be.

"In Jamaica, education isn't free," he told me once. "Secondary schooling costs a lot, and you're damned lucky if your family's able to afford it. No one screws around there because it's such a privilege to get your education. Not true of American kids. They take it for granted." In spite of my abiding belief in the importance of free education, there was no denying Callum had a point. Though his power to do anything about it was limited, his tolerance for his classmates' antics was even lower than mine.

———

I taught Callum for eleventh- and twelfth-grade AP English. I wanted him to try applying to a top-notch school, maybe in the Ivy League, or at the very least, to get out of the city. No such luck; Callum's father— who had sired eighteen or nineteen children, by Callum's count—lived in Jamaica, so Callum's mom and sisters relied on him as the "man of the house." He was staying put. He enrolled at one of the CUNY schools and began studying a combination of Japanese and psychology.

At first, college seemed to be working out pretty well for him. While he was quick in any conversation to point out self-deprecatingly, "it's not like I'm attending the world's best college," the truth was that Callum was making friends, enjoying his classes, and joining student groups. He was even learning to play pool. (This made me laugh, because he was the least likely pool-shark I could imagine.)

He and I kept in touch mostly by Google-chat. We were both night owls, and it was a rare week wherein we didn't end up talking online at least two or three times, if only to send each other YouTube videos we liked. During academic holidays, we'd meet up, usually on the Upper West Side. We'd go eat lunch somewhere, maybe a diner—or, alternately, I'd make Callum his favorite "Jewish" sandwich of lox with a bit of lemon-juice and butter on pumpernickel bread with a salad on the side. Then we'd amble leisurely through the park, sometimes stopping so I could run an errand, and usually end up at the giant Barnes & Noble on East Eighty-Sixth Street, where we'd read comics together for the rest of the afternoon. Other times he'd come over, we'd eat, and then he'd help me move furniture in my apartment, or fix my computers, or do any number of other quasi-chores for me that were really more of an excuse for us to hang out together than anything that actually needed doing.

Callum was eighteen or nineteen by the time we were able to be friends this way; I was about twenty-six. Even if we had been romantically involved, it would've been legal. We weren't—yet, I still sometimes felt freaked out that someone might perceive things that way. By Callum's nature, he was something of a flirt: He would tell me I had pretty eyes or remind me of the fact that a group of boys in his class had apparently shared some sort of fantasies about me. I found this information, which I had not known at the time, simultaneously flattering and horrifying in the ways it could possibly be misconstrued by anyone who might overhear our conversation. I would beg, "Shhh! Enough out of you!" when he'd say these things (to which he would burst out laughing); I worried someone would see *my* intentions as predatory in some way.

Our friendship was pure. In my years of teaching, Callum is the only student with whom I felt, eventually, that a certain type of equality and understanding existed between us, such that we could be true peers. I still advised him on all manner of things, from which courses to take, to how to deal with awkward situations with his various girlfriends. However, I felt my ability to do this was merely the consequence of a few more years spent on earth—a sort of "been there, done that" type of expertise. In turn, I shared my interests and dreams with him. I let him read things I'd written. We never ceased to crack each other up. As I get further in age from the students that I teach (who, despite my increasing years, are always the same age when I get them), I realize the opportunities to become true friends with any students are dwindling, such that I'm not sure I'll ever form a friendship like this again with any one of them.

————

In the beginning of his sophomore year of college, Callum's progress came to a sudden halt. Until then, he'd been getting straight A's and enjoying college life. Suddenly, he was getting D's and F's. His professors, he recounted to me, were supportive, but concerned; several of them had asked if he wanted to retake tests or had assured him without his prompting, "Just so you know, I'll drop your lowest grade. . . ." He talked about changing schools to somewhere with a fencing team; I was confused, as he'd never before expressed an iota of interest in fencing. Our late night Google-chat conversations were morose. "I guess I should do my statistics homework, but I'm tired," he'd say. And then he wouldn't do it. Not even late. That semester, he failed three courses and barely passed the fourth, which was Japanese.

He was always straightforward with me about what was going on. He told me when he failed tests he should've been acing, skipped out on labs that he knew would determine his final grades. His GPA was crashing and burning, and he never tried to hide it from me. He'd seem alternately anxious ("This is really bad, right?") and apathetic ("I just can't bring myself to care") when I would speak to him about it.

I was alarmed. I knew his mother had been very sick, and though she had improved by the end of that year, it became apparent that the very fact of her illness had taken a blow on Callum's psyche. Somehow, I found this unexpected, though I don't know why I did: She was the only parent he had in the country, a rock upon which he'd built his life in ways I hadn't realized. It occurred to me, during that season, that I had never truly considered her role in helping form the incredible young man Callum had turned out to be. Confronting her failing health had left him shaken and deeply depressed.

"You can never have a semester like this again," I told him over Christmas vacation, with a look that I hoped conveyed both serious-ness and concern. I scrutinized him from across plates of eggs, toast, and turkey bacon. (We were at a diner again.) "I'm worried for you, kiddo."

"I know." He looked dejectedly down at his food. He had dark circles under his eyes and appeared gaunt. He had lost weight off his already skinny frame. "Believe me, I know."

———

He turned it around. Reconciled to the inevitability that he would have to graduate at least a semester later than the rest of his peers due to the fact that he now had to retake several critical courses for his major, Callum plunged himself into the spring semester determined to take on the world. I never knew what reserves of strength he pulled from (other than school-provided counseling) or if anything specific had caused his depression to lift. I can only report my observation that, after the break, Callum was ready to go. His apathy gone (and, I suspect, his pride somewhat wounded), he became a more determined student than before. Very soon, he was again pulling straight A's.

It was during the first semester of his junior year that I had the idea of Callum writing for *Dissent Magazine*, a leftist rag begun by some Brandeis professors in the 1950s that focused on cultural, social, and political issues with a liberal bent. I'd been writing for *Dissent*, as well, and now they were doing a series called "30 Under Thirty." I suspected Callum, now twenty, might be a good fit.

Callum was assigned to write an article about how family had, in some way, pushed him towards education. He pondered it for a while and then sent me a first draft (I was assigned to edit for him) that was part memoir, part polemic. "Imagine running a marathon in which most of the other runners actively try to hold you back if you are going too fast. They congratulate you when you are running as slowly as they are; not winning is the thing to do," it read. "Going to public school in the Bronx is just like that."

I cringed. His anger at his peers, while justified, was never going to work for the magazine; I knew they were looking for a more upbeat story of triumph over obstacles. But moreover, seeing his frustration expressed so starkly filled me with retroactive guilt for my role in his experience. Had I been a better disciplinarian, could I have stopped his sense of being held back? Was the feeling of being congratulated for running slowly one that I had inadvertently fostered through my own weaknesses as a young teacher?

I ran it by our editor at the magazine. He was not pleased. "I see that you have got Callum writing wonderfully on a sentence-by-sentence basis. But I worry that he's playing the 'victimized youth,' which isn't interesting. This was to be a piece for a section on how his family relationships influenced his education—and it is really a gripe about schools," he said.

"Should I have him add some things about his family?" I asked.

"Have him start over."

I went back to Callum. I wanted to say, "Hey, are you mad at me? Did I contribute to your feeling of being held back in high school? Should I have been harder on your peers?" and then hear him tell me, no, I'd always supported him, I was the reason he'd succeeded, etc. Then I reasoned that, even if I hadn't been the perfect model of pedagogy, maybe our friendship—as it had become—had moved past whatever slight he might believe I'd allowed to happen to him back in the day.

"Callum," I told him as gently as I could over Google-chat, "Your essay has to be changed a little bit."

"How much is a little bit?"

"Rewritten entirely."

I expected him to get mad. Instead, after a moment he wrote, "Oh no! LOL!"

Bolstered by his good spirits, I explained again what he needed to do: incorporate more family, fewer jibes at former classmates.

"Oh, no problem!" he said. He sounded completely unperturbed. "That's actually easier anyway; I know exactly what I'll write. I'll have it for you in a few days."

His second try was resoundingly better. From the sobering opener— "I'm the seventeenth, eighteenth, possibly nineteenth child of my father. But who's counting? Certainly, he's not."; to the usual self-deprecation— "I haven't ended up at the world's best college . . ."; to the tribute to his mother—"My mother continued to push me, doing whatever it took to make me do well . . . it motivates me that she still cares about my education"; it was pure Callum: occasionally cynical, sometimes brilliant, always real.

One line in particular struck me, near the end: "I have met enough of the positive expectations to avoid being viewed as yet another casualty of the Jamaican or American education systems. In the inner-city middle schools and high school I attended, I often got the sense that my classmates and I were expected to drop out and become failures—join gangs, become teenage parents, etc."[3] I don't know what my expectations of Callum as a student consisted of, back when I was his teacher, beyond his graduating high school and making something of himself— but whatever they were, he has surpassed them and more. He has given me every reason to be proud of him, as his former teacher, as his sometimes editor, and as his friend.

---

3   From the article "Mom, Dad, College, and Me," *Dissent Magazine*, December 2011.

CHAPTER SIXTEEN

Ilana

In my second or third year of teaching, when I was around twenty-three, I went on a blind date. It was a disaster from the outset—the guy and I had nothing in common other than both being Jewish, and he kept trying to impress me by saying things like "What were your SAT scores? I bet mine were higher."

I had asked him about his job, and now he returned the volley. "I teach high school English," I told him.

"Where?" He guessed the name of a local Jewish private school.

"No, it's public school—in the Bronx."

He looked surprised. "Wow, I bet the bullets just whiz over your head every minute!" he quipped.

It was a remark I could have seen myself making jokingly in the company of friends, especially other Bronx teachers; indeed, at that very moment I had on my wall a cartoon clipped from the New York Post, in which some soldiers are pictured sitting in a trench, explosions all around, with the caption: "Hey, things could be worse . . . we could be students in a New York City public school. . . ."

But when he said it, something in me recoiled.

You don't understand at all, I wanted to tell him. *How dare you say that about my students.*

Instead I said meekly, "No, it isn't really very unsafe." I never called him again.

I think it was around that time that the affinity I had developed for the students dawned on me. It wasn't merely the kids themselves, though they were generally delightful; I could have seen myself falling in love with a group of kids in a magnet school or a private school just as easily. Rather, it was the sense of doing work that was concrete, interactive, of knowing that it would matter to someone if I didn't show up one morning. I felt infinitely protective of the kids. It seemed to me that they had been slighted in more ways than I could enumerate, while my peers and I had been given ever more incalculable advantages over them. To say I felt guilty isn't quite accurate; it was more that I had become sort of single-mindedly focused on trying to make up to them the things I felt they had unjustly missed.

That, and I liked teaching. "It's addictive," one of my mentors told me, "because it's so f—ing hard. And when you do it successfully, it's a high . . . it feels amazing."

Boy, was she right.

———

I think I took it as a given that I would leave at some point—mostly because I wanted desperately to go back to school. I loved reading and learning. Post high school, I even loved being in class. I wasn't sure what discipline I wanted to undertake, exactly. I felt a pull towards a PhD program in English literature, as I had considered doing in college, but after nearly four years of teaching in the Bronx, the idea had begun to lose its luster. What could I say about Chaucer that no one had already said before? What could I do that would really be productive?

It was the students who helped me to figure it out. I was teaching a creative writing class titled Creative Nonfiction and the Personal Narrative—one I had invented on the spot during my interview over a year prior, when asked what elective I would teach if given the choice. The course requirements involved writing weekly one- to two-page assignments from a variety of prompts. I believe the first one was a memoir prompt—something vaguely along the lines of "an important incident in your life."

"Will you do it with us?" one of the kids asked. The others immediately chimed in, "Yeah! You have to do it with us!"

It hadn't occurred to me that they would be remotely interested in hearing my writing. "Sure, I guess," I told them.

I wrote a story for them about my best high school friend (and unrequited crush), Edmund, who had gotten into a car accident when he and I were both sixteen. He had fallen asleep at the wheel and killed another driver. I tried to tell the story in a way that conveyed how I had felt at sixteen—the age that my students were now. I read it aloud to them that Friday, and for once they were silent.

"Miss," said one of the boys, Carl. "You should write a book."

I had never thought about it until that moment. I knew I found writing cathartic, at the very least; in fact, I had been crafting small stories about my teaching experiences, as well as keeping copious journals, ever since my first days in Explorers. But I didn't think I was creative enough. Now, I shrugged off Carl's suggestion. A book? Me? What could I possibly write about?

"You should," said Carl, persistently. "You should write a book for teenagers. I'd read it."

The seed was planted in my head, and several months of consideration did nothing to dislodge it. It was true—I liked writing. It was what I had always done instinctively, absent any course telling me to, when I had wanted to process anything I was having trouble with. So, I thought, "What the hell?" I sent in three stories I had written, all about teaching, to a few MFA programs in the New York area. To my surprise, I was accepted to all but one.

I told the kids I would be graduating with them. For the seniors, this made perfect sense; they were on their way out anyway. The sophomores had a harder time with it.

"Are you leaving because you hate us?" they asked plaintively.

I felt horrible when they said things like that—like I was yet another adult abandoning them. Teaching in the Bronx was, in some ways, like watching a car accident, I had realized: You couldn't just turn away once you had seen the grim spectacle of inner-city education. And here I was preparing to do just that.

"No, that's not it at all! I love you guys—I mean it! I just . . . I'm in my mid-twenties, and it's a convenient time for me to go to graduate school and get my master's."

"Why can't you do it after we graduate?"

"Well . . . at some point, I'm going to want to settle down, have kids of my own, that sort of thing . . . and I'll want to be finished with school by then."

"You can have kids right now!" they protested.

I was floundering. "Right, but I want to be able to focus on being a mom when I have kids—it will be harder to do it if I'm a student still." I said this very deliberately, with the hopes that some of the girls were listening. "And that means I have to get this graduate school stuff done *before* I get married or start having a family."

Comprehension seemed to dawn on them. "Ohhh," they said. "You go do that, Miss." I wondered what I had said that suddenly clarified everything.

I found out a month later, when cards started appearing on my desk saying things like "We will miss you! Good luck with the wedding!" They never said anything about graduate school.

————

They threw me a surprise good-bye party at the end of May. It had been planned for after school, but whoever had been in charge of luring me into the classroom where the kids were waiting had clearly fallen down on the job. One of the boys, Pablo, came to get me in the teacher's lounge. "They're trying to surprise you, but you were supposed to know where to go," he said, looking dismayed. "The girls are all crying now."

"Oh my goodness—I'm sorry."

I followed Pablo to the room and walked in. There were about twenty-five kids in the room. The girls were crying, just as Pablo had said.

"Guys! I'm here! It's okay!"

"You're leaving!"

"Geez, I'm not dying! The school year doesn't end for another month—and after that, I'll be teaching summer school as well, so you'll see me there!" I said. "And what's more, I'm not leaving the city—any of you can come see me whenever you want. Just take the 2 train down to Ninety-Sixth Street. Seriously. I'll buy you all lunch."

It was no use. They were inconsolable. One of the guys grimly cut into the cake—a strawberry jam-filled confection with butter cream icing. We ate it in near silence, with isolated whimpering throughout the room. It was the saddest party I had ever had.

———

On the last day of school for teachers—the kids didn't have to come in anymore—I was cleaning out my classroom. I took the posters down from the wall, folded the ones that were salvageable, and put the rest in the garbage. I stacked the remaining homework folders, whose owners had forgotten to collect them, and made a mental note to leave them in the principal's office in case the kids wanted to claim them in the fall.

I looked around my classroom. Without the kids' work on the wall, their colorful hand-drawn posters, and the big WELCOME TO ENGLISH 4 sign, the room looked cavernous and unfamiliar.

I felt a lump in my throat. *It's okay*, I told myself. *You'll see most of them in summer school anyway. And then you'll remember how annoying they can be. It'll be fine.*

It took me a while to sufficiently blink back tears so I could go into the hallway where the other teachers were hanging out.

———

I taught summer school, and then I went back to school—this time as a student. I spent the next two years writing mostly stories about my experiences being a teacher in the Bronx. I kept in touch with many of the kids—in the age of Facebook, Google-chat, and email, I discovered it was pretty easy to keep tabs on them, and not only because I was still writing college recommendations for half of them.

The week before each break, I would make a point to travel up to the school and see them: Usually I would come in at their lunchtime and go downstairs to the cafeteria, where I would join them. They would jump all over me until I begged for air. Then we would take cell phone pictures (totally against the rules of the school, which forbade students from bringing in cell phones), and someone would usually "buy me a drink"—a can of juice from the vending machine. I would escort them back to their classes at the end of lunch, say hi to some of the teachers, and then head home. I always left feeling really loved. It was impossible to deny how much I missed teaching and how much I missed them.

———

In the spring of 2009, I prepared to leave the two-year MFA program and reenter the working world. Though I was beginning to write professionally, my plan was to return to teaching as my main source of income, at least for the foreseeable future—and I was glad about this. I had missed the classroom. I interviewed at a bunch of different schools: some charter, some private, some new public "small schools" with themes like gaming, or arts, or "green" living. None of them seemed quite right. I wanted to work near where I was living—I hated the commute to the Bronx—but I wasn't finding a place where I was particularly comfortable.

So, I emailed the principal of the small school I had worked at on the Explorers campus. It was a new principal now—she was smart, organized, and had a great reputation for being supportive of teachers.

"It's really improved from when you were there," Dan told me when I asked. He was still teaching biology. Most of the teachers I liked were still there, as well.

The principal and I talked. She offered me the opportunity to teach the courses I wanted, the late schedule I wanted, and perhaps most importantly, the feeling that I myself was wanted. The commute started to seem less insurmountable. *Maybe I could move closer to Ninety-Sixth Street*, I told myself. "Just let me know in the next couple of months," the principal said.

The students knew I was up there; some of my former sophomores, now seniors, were milling around in the hallway as I exited the principal's office.

"You're coming back here, aren't you?" someone asked.

"I knew it! Miss Garon! How you gonna come back right when we graduate? That's wack!"

"Guys. Chill. I have no big announcements to make," I said flatly.

"Yeah right. We know what's up. Pablo told us you're coming back."

"What? Since when is Pablo privy to my professional decisions?"

"Whatever. Come on! Tell us! Are you coming back, or what?"

I walked towards the exit. I was smiling.

CONCLUSION

Final Thoughts

A group of students I taught a few years ago had a game they liked to play with me after school: They'd hang out in my classroom messing about while I cleaned up or graded papers, sometimes making half-hearted attempts at their own homework, and all the while try to persuade me that I should call one of them "n—ah."

"Come on, Miss!" the ringleader would say. They'd all be gathered around my desk by this point, barely able to contain their laughter, and the ringleader would always be pointing to some equally game friend. (Not all of them were black, either—apparently, you could belong to any of the ethnic groups represented in our school and find this game hilarious.) "Just say it once! Say it to him, 'Hey, n—ah!' or 'N—ah, please'—he'll answer you!"

I'd look at them warily, bemused by their regular insistence that I *had* to do this. "Guys. You know there's no situation in which it's *remotely* okay for me to use that word," I'd tell them.

"Come on! Just once! No one here's gonna tell. Right guys?" And they'd all immediately concur—"Yeah, sure, Miss! Doesn't leave this room!"

I never took the bait. It wasn't that I doubted they'd keep their promises; I truly believe this group of kids both liked me, but I was keenly aware of the trouble I would face as a teacher if I were ever legitimately accused of using such racially charged language in everyday conversation.

But to me, it would have felt too uncomfortable. Even in the sense that they were using it and were encouraging me to use it—emphasizing the last syllable not as the Jim Crow–era "n—ER," but "n—ah," which was closer to "dude" in their parlance than it was to a pejorative term for blacks—the whole idea seemed unequivocally wrong in my eyes. I just couldn't get around the fact that, no matter how comfortable I was with this bunch of kids, my saying the "n-word" as a white teacher to mostly black and Latino students would in some way give life to a vicious system of thought that needed to be put to rest.

I've thought of this series of interactions many times, in trying to articulate the ideas behind this collection. In relating my experience teaching in the Bronx, it seems naïve to ignore the reality of my being suburban, middle-class, and white. To the extent that tolerance, connectedness, and even affection has existed between my students and me—and I do believe that I've had that rapport with many students—it has never been under a pretense of "sameness" or of overlooking the vast disparities that have existed and continue to exist in our backgrounds. In most cases, I believe the students saw and continue to see me as a sort of bewildered traveler in their world; they grasp that I am eager to understand, experience, and know my way around, yet I am already far too displaced from it all to do anything but emphathize with what daily life as an inner-city student entails. In short, I'll never be a permanent resident.

In recent years, it seems that everyone has developed a theory about "what's wrong" with inner-city schools. From poor teaching (including the idea that teacher tenure facilitates an inherent disincentive to improve), to lack of technological resources, to the need for more standardized tests, most of the theories proposed have failed to take into account the challenges faced by students like the ones whom I've taught.

I would submit that poverty itself is the issue within inner-city schools. As far back as elementary school, the students I've taught are already, in many cases, at an incalculable disadvantage compared to their wealthier peers. They know fewer words when they start school. They read far less frequently at home, no doubt because in the process of working two to three jobs to support a family, their parents simply have less time at home to support their literacy skills. They have been babysat by the television and (more recently) the Internet all too frequently, to the point where the intellectual effort required to read a novel or solve a math problem becomes a frustrating delay in gratification—if there is no immediate pay-off (in literature, that means graphic sex or violence within the first few pages), the kids become bored. They come to school hungry, tired, without eyeglasses. Whether this is an issue of economics—they cannot afford food or eyeglasses or had to work late supporting the family and thus got no sleep—or whether this is simply parental inattention, I'm not sure. The issue of "fault" is irrelevant when the effect is the same: The students come to school emotionally and physically unprepared to learn.

In the direst situations, these students have been bereft of parenting altogether; they've been raised in foster homes, or by siblings not much older than themselves. They dodge family cycles of abuse, teen preg-nancy, drugs and alcohol, involvement in gang activity, and jail time. While it would be a gross generalization to imply that this is the norm, it must be said that I've seen these situations far too many times. To expect that the students who endure these crises can regularly come to school, quietly sit down at their desks, and turn in their homework without incident—ignoring the reality of their lives outside of school— is absurd; the only thing more shocking is that sometimes they actually *do* manage this herculean task.

———

I cannot suggest any one single panacea for these ills, but I do think that recognizing their economic underpinnings is key to coming up with a relevant solution. And I don't think the solution can be addressed solely through inner-city classrooms, as what happens there is merely a symptom of the greater problem; rather, we need to elevate entire families—make Head Start programs widely available; offer healthier (and better-tasting) school breakfasts and lunches; provide lower-cost, post-secondary education options; build opportunities to learn and work at skilled trades starting at the high school level and continuing into adulthood (through community colleges and factory-based trade programs); and empower community-based organizations.

The culture of education also is due for a change, and that's not something that's more pertinent to my students than to their peers in wealthier districts. However churlish it may be to say this, it must be mentioned that the prevailing trend is one wherein students—and this applies particularly to those at the high school level—are no longer held accountable by the adults around them for their own educational progress. It is common for students to misbehave by talking incessantly, cursing, or fighting in class, and these disruptions (which set back not only the disruptive students, but also their classmates) are seen as normal occurrences in inner-city schools, even in high school, even in students as old as eighteen.

I always find it particularly eye-opening to view this trend through the eyes of students who are not American-born, who are frankly shocked and offended by the behavior of their classmates. "These kids take education for granted," more than one of them has told me. "They ruin class for the rest of us, and their parents and school officials just let them get away with it." Administrators at every level, from the school to the state, have failed to set consequences for such misbehavior; for instance, expulsion from public school is illegal in New York State, and students can go so far as to "curse out" a teacher without receiving a suspension, as a result of legislation designed not to "deprive students of their education." Punitive systems are problematic in their own right, but so are systems wherein poor citizenship goes unchastened and uncorrected.

Too many of the parents are inclined to blame the fact that their children "don't like the teachers" or "aren't interested in the material" before considering their own responsibilities to instill discipline within their families. But there comes a point when blaming the teacher for poor instruction, or the class for not being "engaging" enough, ceases to be relevant. Certainly, parents and guardians must act in support and protection of students, promoting their best interests. But to fail to hold them accountable for their own success—as students and as human beings—is to promote a culture of failure, and ultimately, to subvert them as masters of their own futures.

––––––––

It becomes difficult to talk about the problems of inner-city education without acknowledging the fact that poverty and race are so inextricably linked in this country. I was once trying to explain to the owner of a bar—who was, herself, African American—that my students would have trouble with Toni Morrison's *Beloved*, a book she was suggesting I teach, in its more ponderous sections.

"But why?" she exclaimed. "Don't you think they'd get behind the idea of an African American author and protagonists?" She seemed offended that I wasn't going to try it on my tenth-graders. "Are you saying you don't think they could *handle* it?"

I had trouble conveying to her that the issues they'd have with the book weren't about identifying with the characters, and moreover, that their issues connecting with different novels didn't really have anything to do with the skin color of the protagonists. Then there was the question of reading level (I myself read *Beloved* in twelfth-grade AP English, while my students were only in tenth grade); even their peers two years older would have trouble with a book of such complexity. And my assessment that they would likely struggle with *Beloved* wasn't me thinking, *Black kids can't handle such a difficult book.* It was, *Kids with low literacy skills will struggle with such a difficult book.*

Even if I were so inclined, I couldn't attribute my students' academic troubles more directly to any particular ethnic group than any other; there are kids of every different background in our school building. The majority are either Latino and black—American, from island nations like Jamaica, or from Africa. But a sizeable portion of my students are also from the Balkan nations. Then there are some who are Asian, some who are Italian, and some whose origins I can't even guess. I see no discernible correlation between race and academic achievement in this school—there are top-notch students and students who struggle from every background. The common denominator that brings them to my classroom with reading skills that haven't been well-developed *isn't* their race; it's their language gaps, their interrupted formal education, the distractions they face at home, and the underlying culprit of it all, their poverty. That's what keeps them from engaging with a text like *Beloved*, but I sometimes think that saying so is akin to blasphemy.

———————

In reading this book, some will certainly accuse me of perpetuating stereotypes everyone would rather avoid—ideas of minority students who are disruptive, fail to take advantage of opportunities, and do not succeed in overcoming the obstacles in front of them. I would argue that my goal has been to present a range of experiences (though some of them are undoubtedly cynical) that show the problems, joys, successes, and surprises presented by the students in an inner-city school. To whatever extent possible, I've tried to avoid "white washing" the situation, or as one of my mentors once cautioned me, to avoid presenting a "Pollyanna" approach to life in an inner-city school.

Does this make me racist or unsympathetic? I hope not. I would like to think that the fact that I have worked in the Bronx public schools for nearly ten years now gives me license to talk frankly and honestly about what I've seen, even if it doesn't present the vision most outsiders would like to see.

I feel confident in asserting that my students would share this view. They would say that if I were to ignore the issues at hand, or to downplay the difference between what I'd like to see and what actually happens, I'd be acting in a disingenuous way. "Do *you*," they always exhort me. "Just do *you*." That's the method I've tried to apply here.

My intention has never been to be prescriptive, or even idealistic, so much as realistic. I don't have the answers. I'm not sure who does. This book is intended to be expository, to show what it is to be in these schools on a daily basis as a young, inexperienced teacher, and a high school student. To the extent that this book is more tragedy than comedy, that is a reflection of what is, rather than what I hope (and anyone who wishes to change education hopes) that the future might bring.

Lastly, I continue to believe in the institution of public school, against all odds. Free education may be the best thing America has to offer, and to whatever extent we can improve its quality and its efficacy in enabling our students to lead meaningful, productive lives, we must continue striving as a society to do so.

Epilogue

Where Are They Now?

I have lost touch with some of the students, especially the ones from my first two years. Here are the ones I have been able to keep track of, either personally, through other teachers, or through Facebook:

STUDENTS

Carlos lives in New York. He has a girlfriend, works, and attends community college.

Alex moved to Puerto Rico.

Kayron left Explorers, earned a GED, and currently attends one of the four-year colleges in the City University of New York (CUNY) system.

Felicia graduated from Explorers and enrolled in one of the CUNY schools.

Jonah lives and works in New York City. He has a girlfriend and has become a devout Catholic.

Adam began his college career at a private college in the Midwest, where he had a full scholarship, but left after two years. He is finishing school at one of the CUNY schools and working part-time.

Destiny enrolled in a high school with a nursery, from which she graduated.

Tyler is attending one of the State University of New York (SUNY) schools in upstate New York, at which he hopes to play football.

Tonya graduated from a private college in upstate New York, where she had a full scholarship and majored in dance. She is months away from completing an MFA in poetry.

Callum graduated from one of the CUNY schools, and is now working in a psychology lab and studying for his GREs. He plans to study psychology at the graduate level.

FACULTY

Alice still works in the small school as a social worker.

Dan still teaches biology, but in a public high school in a different neighborhood.

Ilana is still teaching. She is now in her ninth year in the NYC school system.

Acknowledgments

There are so many people without whom this book would never have been possible—and now I'm going to tell you a little bit about them all, in no particular order. Nicolaus Mills, at Sarah Lawrence College, was the first person to ask, when I showed him a story about teaching, "Do you have more of these?" He made me see that the sum of my experiences could be a book, and then pushed me to stop navel-gazing and make it happen. Nick—the *Talmud* says to find yourself a friend and teacher; you've been both.

Other teachers at the Sarah Lawrence MFA program who helped me variously to shape this book are Gerry Albarelli, Susan Cheever, Lee Edwards, and Jo Ann Beard. All of them encouraged me to take risks as a writer. I am deeply grateful. At Barnard College, before I even knew I was "creative," Anne Prescott, Timea Szell, and Peter Platt pushed me to be a better English student and to love the printed word; through their efforts, they informed my reading, my writing, and my teaching.

I would not have started writing without the encouragement of Eli Muller, who brow-beat me into submitting my first articles to the school newspaper at age sixteen, and then kept brow-beating me for sixteen more years to keep doing that. Jora Stixrud LaFontaine and Rachel Prunier, two of the most accomplished women and best friends I've ever known, have offered me inspiration to achieve my goals and reassurance in times I needed a friendly voice. Scott Jones gave me computer tech support, cold beer, a filing system, and helped me to feel "like a boss" again whenever shyness or self-doubt got in my way. I love all of you.

I also love my strong, beautiful Barnard (and Columbia) women: Ilana Greenberg Kurizki (my name twin and friendship lobster), Chava Brandriss (who also taught in the trenches with me), Adrienne Rose, Tami Wallenstein, Batsheva Glatt, Laetia Kress, and Marla Lemonik all saw me as a writer before I ever did.

I couldn't have written half this many chapters without the butt-kicking and feedback of my mega-talented writer-friends: Jeanne Alnot, Adrienne Friedberg, Adam Chandler, Barbara McGuire, Maris James, Lillian Ho, Mike Stutzman, Mira Ptacin, Emily Zemler, Bernadette McComish, Aaron Epstein, Avi Mermelstein, and especially Michael Robin, who read or listened to umpteen drafts of each of these stories, and helped me to make them better in ways that I couldn't have thought of on my own. At the same time, my "OTP"—Original Teacher Posse— lived through the trials and tribulations recorded herein with me. Arlene Yiadom-Daley, Matt Daley, David Wade, Jenny Rosenthal, Kristina Kirtley, Ben Caraballo, and Robert Harrits helped me see humor amidst many frustrating situations, and showed me how to be a better teacher through their examples.

Nicole Frail at Skyhorse Publishing took a chance on a book with a crazy title and, in doing so, helped me to fulfill a giant life goal. Her eagle-eyed reading and incisive suggestions have made this book better in every way, and her patient fielding of my many frantic emails has helped me to be a more sane person. She is everything a writer could want in an editor. Thanks also to Danielle Ceccolini who created a fun, awesome, and quirky cover for this book—it is a perfect visual representation of everything contained herein.

Family is everything. My cousin and de-facto sister, Becky Cooper Nadis (a.k.a. the "best lover of my fun") helped me to "workshop" these stories in her living room, and usually fed me dinner. Aunt Sally, Uncle Bruce, Aunt Ilka, Uncle Fred, Aunt Carolyn, Uncle Herb, and cousins

Lisa, Ben, and Dina, as well as numerous other members of my huge family, have been faithful readers and Facebook promoters of anything I've sent them, and brought me everything from Persian cucumbers to article clippings to knitted wool hats.

Lastly, my immediate family: My wonderful and witty brothers, Haskell, Jonathan, and Isaac Garon, with whom I share cherished memories of everything from full-contact chess, to toiling in the Virginia sun for $0.05 a weed, to joining a family cell phone plan. There are no "snakes" next to whom I'd rather fall asleep in synagogue than you guys. Mom and Dad, you are the very pillars of my life, which you have helped me to build through your love, encouragement, promotion of literacy (along with other good life skills!), and willingness to take my phone calls at 2 a.m. My gratitude is endless, and I love you more than I can say.